FORTY YEARS A SPECULATOR:

MY DISCOVERIES AND INSIGHTS

By: Fred Carach

ISBN: 978-1-4303-1660-2

CONTENTS

FORTY YEARS A SPECULATOR:

MY DISCOVERIES AND INSIGHTS

I am not a Wall Street professional. In real life I am retired military and a State Certified General Real Estate Appraiser. I made my first investment in 1961 at the age of nineteen and have been addicted to the market ever since. In more than forty years as a speculator and investor, I have purchased over 500 securities. With the exception of commodities, I have purchased every type of financial investment that there is. Stock, bonds, junk bonds, convertible bonds,convertible preferred stocks, options,warrants, and a long time favorite, penny mining stocks.

The catalyst that started this work was that in the bear market years of 2000, 2001, and 2002 when everyone else was losing money, my stock picks were shooting the lights out. And I knew why! The stocks that I owned were radically different from what the touts were promoting. The hard-learned knowledge that I had acquired over more than four decades as an investor had resulted in a stock portfolio of well over a hundred names that neither the touts nor any of my friends had ever heard of. I knew I lived in an investment world that is strange and wondrous, a world that is totally alien from the world of Wall Street and its touts. I am the anti-blue-chip investor and the advocate of small-cap and micro-cap investing.

In the beginning,like everyone else, I bought big capitalization blue-chip stocks. After all, isn't that what you are supposed to buy? As the years progressed I realized that big caps weren't the answer. They couldn't be, they were way too expensive and they didn't move. I needed stocks that I could easily buy in massive amounts, in blocks of hundreds of shares and indeed thousands of shares, and big-cap stocks selling for $50 or $60 a share weren't the answer. On top of that I discovered that stocks in this price range didn't move, at least not the way I wanted them to move. A stock selling for $60 a share that went up 15% or 20% in a great year wasn't going to make it for me. And in a bad year, forget it! These Godzillas don't move! I wanted stocks that would go to the moon.

As the years progressed, I gradually found what I was looking for in the unknown, hidden, and unreported world of small-cap and micro-cap investing. Allow me to introduce you to my world; a strange amalgam of investor, speculator, and dare I say it, riverboat gambler. In a world in which most investors are deliriously happy to earn a rinky-dink 15% a year, I shoot for the moon, and I hit it more often than most people would believe possible. Stick around and I will show you how it is done. What follows has been hard learned over many years as an investor and is an introduction to my world.

To be successful in investing you must understand Wall Street and how it thinks. The apple of Wall Street's eye is, and always has been, big-cap growth. Wall Street divides all stocks into three size categories, big capitalization stocks, mid capitalization stocks and small capitalization stocks. Capitalization is computed by multiplying the stock's price by the number of shares outstanding. The kings of big-cap growth are called the "Nifty Fifty". There is no official list of the "Nifty Fifty" as there is of the Dow Jones Industrials or the S&P 500, but everyone on Wall Street knows what is on the list. To be on the "Nifty Fifty", a stock must be a member of the S&P 500, and it is always one of the 100 largest capitalization stocks in the S&P 500, and it is generally the case that it is one of the 50 largest capitalization stocks in the S&P 500.

In about thirty days you can learn all of the "Nifty Fifty" stocks just by watching CNBC News, the financial news channel. You will quickly discover that the same 50 stocks' names will be repeated again and again and again. These are the "Nifty Fifty". The "Nifty Fifty", and to a lesser extent the S&P 500 - which by itself constitutes an amazing 77% of total stock market capitalization - dominate Wall Street to a degree that is astounding. You are probably wondering what the capitalization of the notorious Dow Jones Industrials is; these 30 dinosaurs constitute an amazing 25% of total stock market capitalization.

In the United States there is a total universe of about 17,000 publicly traded stocks that report to the SEC, and about 10,000 of these are traded daily. The remaining 7,000 aren't regarded by Wall Street as being liquid enough, and many tend to trade "by appointment only", as the saying goes, and are almost always ignored unless you are a micro-cap specialist. You would never know that there were 10,000 tradable stocks by following Wall Street. At its most generous, Wall Street recognizes 3,000 stocks. These are divided into two groups called the Russell 1000 Index, which is a list of the 1,000 largest capitalization stocks in the country and which accounts for 91% of total stock market capitalization; and the Russell 2000 Index, which consists of the next 2000 largest capitalization stocks. In its most recent configuration, the largest corporation in the Russell 1000 had a market capitalization of a staggering $487 billion, and the smallest had a capitalization of $1.4 billion. Wall Street almost never ventures below this capitalization. The smaller cap Russell 2000 is only known to Wall Street through hearsay. No serious investor would consider investing in these stocks, and the remaining universe of 7,000 stocks exists in a black hole and never appears on Wall Street's radarscope. The only exception to this is the small handful of mutual funds that are designated small-cap and micro-cap mutual funds. Their influence on the Street is minimal.

There are thousands of stock analysts that track the Nifty Fifty and the S&P 500. However, what is truly remarkable is the fact that there are thousands of small caps and micro caps that aren't followed by a single analyst. It is common for a Wall Streeter to spend 40 years on the Street and to never have owned a stock that is not a member of the Nifty Fifty.

THE MYTH OF BIG-CAP GROWTH

Wall Street's most cherished myth is the myth of big-cap growth. It has strict requirements for growth stocks. To be considered a growth stock on Wall Street a stock must grow at a sustained rate of at least 15% per year for a sustained period of years. How tough is this? It is very tough. Let's consider how fast the United States grows. Since its founding, the U.S. has grown at an average real growth rate after inflation of about 3.2% a year. If you add inflation of about 3.5 % a year, you are at about 6.5 %. Even in the historic boom years between 1996 and 1999, when the economy was smoking, the growth rate was only 4.1 %, 4.1 %, 4.7 %, and 4.6 % respectively. This is as good as it gets.

According to data listed on Yahoo's finance section, in the forty year period from 1961 to 2001, in the S&P 500, which is usually used as a proxy for the stock market, both earnings and stock prices advanced roughly 7% a year on average, not including dividends. This doesn't seem like much until you realize the awesome power of compounding over 40 years. The total gain is an amazing 1,500%. During the last 30 years the market has advanced on average about 8% a year, not including dividends, for a total advance of about 1,000%. Thus, historically the average big-cap stock has increased both its earning and its stock price at a rate of 7% to 8% a year. To grow at 15% compounded annually for a sustained period is a heroic achievement for any stock, but for a big-cap stock, it is almost a miracle achievement.

Out of the universe of 1000 big-cap stocks, only about 50 stocks, the Nifty Fifty, can manage it for any length of time, and then only with a healthy dose of creative bookkeeping. At 15% compounded your earnings must double every 4.8 years. In 15 years, a company earning $500 million a year would have to grow to a company that is earning $4 billion. Growth rates like this can't be sustained once you reach behemoth size, unless of course it is thought realistic to have earnings the size of the gross domestic product of France. Only on Wall Street is this regarded as being plausible. On January 21, 2002, the highly regarded Barron's Financial Magazine reported the following:

> *Fannie Mae, whose earnings increased 21% to $5.20 last year, is one of only three companies in the S&P 500 that has generated double-digit earnings growth in each of the past 15 years, the two others are Automatic Data Processing and Home Depot, two former members of the double-digit club, Microsoft and Schering-Plough, didn't make the grade in 2001.*

There you have it! Only three companies out of 500 could even grow at 10% for 15 years. If the test had been 15%, they all would have failed. It is noteworthy that even powerful growth companies like Microsoft, Intel, Oracle, Dell Computer, and Cisco failed to make the grade.

THE SMALL-CAP ENIGMA

The question that inevitably presents itself is: why not invest in mid caps, small caps, and micro caps? Ibbotson Research is well known for its research going back to 1926 proving that small caps outperform big caps over any sustained historical period. It is obvious that these companies have the potential to grow at a faster rate than big caps. What has the greater growth potential, an acorn or a mighty oak tree? The question answers itself, unless of course you are on Wall Street, then things become very murky. You have to understand how Wall Street thinks. There is a reason for Wall Street's hostility to small-cap and mid-cap stocks. The center of Wall Street's world isn't the individual investor, but the institutional investor. Institutional investors, by their very nature, must buy and sell in huge amounts quickly without unduly affecting the price of the stock. This is only truly possible in the Nifty Fifty stocks, and to a lesser extent in the S&P 500. This explanation has the virtue of sounding plausible, but it still fudges a very important issue; why do Wall Street professionals need to dump stocks quickly?

THE NEED TO DUMP

Buying and selling small-cap and mid-cap stocks slowly isn't an option for Institutional Investors. They need to dump stocks in huge amounts quickly. The issue is: why? What great harm could come from unloading stocks slowly over a period of several months? A great deal of harm if you understand how the Street works. Not so long ago it was possible for professional money managers to march to their own drummer, to pick out of favor stocks, to make long-term bets, and to think originally. In those days money managers would be given X million dollars and two or three years to show what they could do. In today's brave new world, the report card comes due every quarter, not in two or three years, and your performance is always measured against the S&P 500. This deeply flawed system has ruined any possibility of independent thinking. It has also terminated the possibility of consistently superior results. The days when independent, original thinkers like Warren Buffet, Sir John Templeton, and Peter Lynch could march to their own drummer and make long-term bets based on their superior research and insights are over.

If the report card comes due every 90 days, the only possible investment strategy is trend chasing. You must stampede with the herd or perish. Research, even very good research, is of little value. The basis of all good research is the assumption that the market hasn't fully recognized the future potential of an investment. If the research is good, as time progresses this potential becomes more and more apparent to all, and the result is a rising market value. The question is how much time is required for this process to unfold. Sir John Templeton, the legendary investor and founder of the Templeton Funds, has the answer. He has stated that in a career spanning decades, his investments take about five years to fully work out. During the first year there is a 50-50 chance that the investment will be in the red. In the second and third year it moves solidly into the black, and the fourth and fifth years are the blow out years when the real profits are earned. Anyone who holds an investment for five years will see this pattern repeat time and time again.

The stock market's greatest secret is that it rewards patience more than any other virtue. The classic holding period for an investment is two to five years. This holding period has withstood the test of time. For any holding period of less than two years, good judgment and research - even very good research - is of limited value. There just isn't enough time for the investment to work itself out. Stock market action for periods of less than two years is essentially random. I realize that the reader may challenge this time period and claim that the classic time period should be reduced to as low as one year. I am willing to admit that the period from one to two years is a gray period, however, my research says that one year just isn't long enough, and I bear the scars to prove it. Time after time I have given up on an investment after one year, sold it at a loss and watched it soar in year two.

Pity today's institutional investor every quarter when his report card comes due. He knows that his best chance for superior performance is to invest in small-cap and mid-cap stocks. But he also knows that such superior performance is only possible in the long-term and not in the short-term. He knows that the benchmark that he will be measured against is the S&P 500, and that in any quarter stock market performance is essentially random. The institutional investor knows that he will be forgiven within reason for big-cap investments that move against him. As the saying goes "no one ever lost their job for picking IBM" no matter how badly it performed.

However, he won't be forgiven for small-cap investments that move against him. Superior research is of little predictive value in a period as short as a quarter. In essence, if the institutional investor is to survive, trend chasing and stampeding with the herd is the only option. No excuse is acceptable for those who don't make their numbers every quarter. They must all dump stocks when they go down and buy stocks when they go up. In short, all must buy and sell Nifty Fifty stocks. Only these stocks meet their needs. Almost without exception the core holding of every large-cap mutual fund is the Nifty Fifty. All are driven by these implacable market forces to chase trends and not to anticipate them. In today's deformed Wall Street jungle only the herd animals survive.

THE RANDOM WALK THESIS

For years one of the Wall Street's most hotly debated controversies has been the "Random Walk Thesis". This thesis, which is also often referred to as the "Efficient Market Hypothesis" or EMH, states that current stock prices reflect all available current information, therefore the stock market is so efficient that it is impossible for investors to outperform the market, and that the market reacts so swiftly to news that only a mathematically insignificant percentage of investors can outperform the "so-called" market averages. Momentum players love this theory; it tells them what they want to believe. It tells them that market research is useless and that the key to successful investing is playing the "earnings expectations" game, guessing which stocks are going to report an "earnings surprise" in the next quarter because that is the only thing that isn't already baked into the cake. The key term here is the "so-called" market averages.

The two major averages are of course the Dow Jones Industrials and the S&P 500. I use the term "so-called" because properly understood the Dow Jones and the S&P 500 are really mutual funds in disguise and not averages. Consider what happened recently when the makeup of the Dow Jones Industrials was changed, as it is from time to time. It dumped its two worst dogs and replaced them with Microsoft and Intel. No one can claim that Microsoft and Intel are average corporations. In short, neither Dow Jones nor Standard & Poor's is really an average; they are in fact mutual funds pretending to be averages. Every time changes are made to these averages, their worst performers are dumped and replaced by the best performing stocks in the big-cap universe.

Given the realities that exist, it can be said that the Random Walk Thesis is correct if you invest in big-cap stocks for holding periods of less than two years. If your holding period is the classic holding period of two to five years, it is far less correct and it breaks down entirely when it comes to small caps that are held for more than two years.

One mutual fund group has ridden to triumph championing the Random Walk Thesis, The Vanguard Mutual Fund Group. Its index mutual funds have swept the big-cap field. Even many so-called managed non-index funds are, if the truth were admitted, so-called "closet index funds" in drag. This can easily be done by artfully buying certain key Nifty Fifty stocks in the correct amounts.

THE INVESTMENT SCHOOLS

Before we get to the troubling matter of day trading, it is important that we analyze the different investment schools that dominate Wall Street. All investors are members of one of the following investment schools whether they know it or not. At this point, before preceding any further, I must declare what must already be obvious. I am of course a small-cap and micro-cap value player. There are only two value schools:

THE FUNDAMENTAL VALUE SCHOOL
THE CONTRARIAN SCHOOL

Perhaps the most important question in investing is: are the rules of investing different in the stock market? Or are they the same universal rules that you would use to analyze the purchase of an income property or a private investor would use to analyze the purchase of an entire business? The above value schools say that there is no difference. The growth schools say that there are major differences, and that the above schools of analysis are flawed.

The fundamental value school is more or less self-explanatory; it involves the rigorous examination of the corporation's income statement and balance sheet in the quarterly reports and the annual statement. Members of this school are called followers of Benjamin Graham and David Dodd, who in 1934 wrote the Bible of fundamental investing called "Security Analysis". Graham later taught finance at Columbia University, where None other than Warren Buffet was his star student. Warren has always felt that the teaching of the great Benjamin Graham was critical to his later investment success.

When I broke into investing more than forty years ago, the followers of Graham and Dodd dominated the stock market. This is no longer the case. As we shall see later on, all the investment schools except the technical analysis school are dominated today by a bastardized form of fundamental analysis which trumpets earnings as the sole determinate of stock value, and relegates the complete and well-rounded analysis championed by Graham and Dodd to oblivion.

The contrarian school is closely related to the value school, and value investors are usually contrarians. The distinction between the two schools is this. Contrarians are far less interested in Graham and Dodd's analysis than they are interested in buying at what Sir John Templeton has called "the point of maximum pessimism". Their specialty is investing in stocks that in Wall Street parlance have " blown up" or "crashed and burned" and are now splattered in the Wall Street gutter. If these stocks were "highfliers" that have "blown up", and they often are, it is very possible that they can still be overpriced on the fundamentals. After the dot.com bubble exploded, it was common to find stocks that had fallen 70%-90% and were still not value plays.

I don't know if Pittsburgh Phil ever owned a stock, but he was a master contrarian. In 1908 he wrote a book that is still in print and revered by horseplayers, *The Racing Maxims of Pittsburgh Phil*. In this classic work one of Pittsburgh Phil's most important maxims was that you should never bet on a horse to do something that it had never done before, or had tried and failed to do. For example, if a horse had run before and won a $25,000 claiming race, then there was a reasonable expectation that it had the potential to win $25,000 claiming races in the future. However, a horse that had tried and failed to win a $25,000 claiming race was a bad bet until it proved it could win a $25,000 claiming race. This is what the contrarian school is all about. A $5.00 stock that used to sell for $25.00 has the potential to sell for $25.00 again as long as the asset base that it had when it was a $25.00 stock is still largely intact. All growth schools are just the opposite. They are always willing to bet that their growth stocks will sell at prices higher than they have ever sold before. Pittsburgh Phil would have told them that whether they are betting on horses or stocks, this is a dangerous game. Below are the growth schools:

THE CLASSICAL GROWTH SCHOOL
GARP
THE MOMENTUM SCHOOLS
TECHNICAL ANALYSIS (CHARTISTS)

These are the "trend chasing" schools. Growth investors are above all else trend chasers and believe that there are only two types of stocks. Stocks that are going up and that therefore are ordained to go up forever, and stocks that are going down and are therefore ordained to go down forever. Growth investors are always shocked when these trends are reversed. They seem to feel that a basic law of the universe has been violated, and they aren't pleased. These schools always have a big following among the "instant self-gratification" crowd. Trend chasing is indeed the road to instant self-gratification until your head is handed to you on a silver platter.

Little needs to be said about the classical growth school. It simply presumes that growth is more profitable than value, and that one is justified in paying a premium for growth. The most interesting and in my opinion the most valid of all growth schools is the GARP school. GARP stands for growth at a reasonable price. This is the only growth school that explicitly states that it is possible to pay too much for growth, and that superior performance results when you don't overpay for growth.

There are two types of momentum schools, and they are closely related: the price momentum school and the earnings momentum school. Their key belief is that stocks with the fastest growing earnings or stocks that display the fastest rise in price, or what is called "relative strength", should be bought blindly and without any regard for value. For those stocks with the greatest momentum, no price can be too high. Given the choice between buying an average stock for ten times earnings or the highest momentum stock at 1,000 times earnings, the momentum player wouldn't hesitate to buy the stock selling at 1,000 times earnings.

There have always been momentum players, but until the 90's they were always small potatoes. The rise of the Random Walk School provided a powerful impetus to their massive growth in the 90's. This school was just what the doctor ordered as far as the momentum players were concerned. It stated that stock analysis was worthless because no one was smart enough to out think the market and that therefore the best policy was to stampede mindlessly with the herd, forever chasing the latest trend. Which is precisely what all momentum players want to believe anyway.

The followers of the Technical Analysis School are often called chartists because of their obsession with charts. They believe that you only need to know two things about a stock, its price and its sales volume. Indeed, one of the founders of this school insisted that his secretary black out the name of the stock charts that he was studying so that he wouldn't be influenced by their names. This school has been around since the 19th Century, but its real popularity began around 1970 when it exploded in popularity. Today the followers of this school are so numerous that they are clearly affecting stock market values, especially when an important top or bottom is penetrated. And this is a very, very big problem for their school, their founders doctrine was that in a world in which fundamental analysis was all-pervasive, the chartists would enjoy a powerful advantage because they were a tiny elite piggybacking on the top of fundamental analysis. Sadly for them, this is no longer the case. Technical analysis is so popular today that in many sectors it is now dominant over fundamental analysis.

The players of this school are now at a big disadvantage, they are poker players who are always showing their hands. These people used to hand make their own charts. Now excellent charts are all over the Internet, and tons of them are free. Indeed I remember reading one of the reports of the great Dow theorist, Richard Russell, in which he complained that he had to fire the person who was making up his daily charts because he discovered that he wasn't learning anything unless he made up the charts himself. Those days are gone. Today nearly everyone uses a handful of standardized charts that are freely available on the Internet; everyone and his brother can now predict how the technicians will act when an important support or resistance line is penetrated. As a value player I find that their charts can be useful as a supporting tool in investment analysis.

DAY TRADERS AND THE MOMENTUM SCHOOL OF INVESTING

There have always been day traders. Historically they were called floor traders. These crafty stock market veterans were the ultimate insiders and owned seats on the New York Stock Exchange. This gave them the enormous advantage of not having to pay commissions on their trades, which is the right of all members of the New York Stock Exchange. When these floor traders closed their positions on the same day that they acquired them, they were called day traders. They provided valuable liquidity to the market.

Today's day traders are a far cry from these crafty veterans. In fact, the most amazing thing about today's day traders is how little they know about the stock market. Most of them acquire what little knowledge they have about it from their day trader's seminar, which is then supplemented by watching CNBC, which has become everyone's default position for financial news. Of course, in all honesty, there isn't a great deal to learn about day trading. Once you have been told that "the trend is your friend" twenty or thirty times, it usually sinks in. From then on it is just a matter of stampeding with the herd. Hunched over your computer screen at the ready to blindly buy any stock with a bullish wire report and sell any stock with a bearish wire report. If you are the fastest gun alive, you can do well, if not, you will be wiped out in short order.

Now it must be understood that while all day traders are momentum players, not all momentum players are day traders. The dean of the momentum school of investing is William J. O'Neil, author of the 1988 book *How to Make Money in Stocks* and the founder of Investors Business Daily newspaper, which is the momentum players' bible. Here you will find stocks ranked by their momentum. The data and detail which you will find in the IBD is very impressive until you realize that what they have done is dressed the "greater fool theory" in a tuxedo and called it momentum investing. The analysis always leads you to the "highfliers" that have broken through to new highs and all to often, all time highs. The theory here is that every holder of the stock is a winner, and therefore there is no overhead resistance of sellers waiting to dump the stock as soon as they get even.

In four decades of investing, the one absolute law that I have discovered is this: every highflier is destined to get blown out of the sky, usually shortly after the stock has been bought by you. There are no exceptions to this law. None.

I have vivid memories of when Polaroid and Xerox were the darlings of the Nifty Fifty. It was claimed that their technology was so superior that they would be highfliers forever. I can remember buying Polaroid when it was selling at a five-year low and taking a vicious loss on this "can't-lose" stock. Polaroid recently declared bankruptcy and Xerox came close to going bankrupt.

Not to worry. O'Neil recommends a safety net of placing a stop-loss order at 7.5% below your buy price. If the stock falls 7.5%, you will be automatically sold out. The problem with this is that every momentum player reads Investors Business Daily, and they are concentrated to an unusual degree in the 15 highest rated stocks. When these stocks disappoint, and in time they will all disappoint, the result isn't the normal price decline, but a cataclysm. Momentum players are the ultimate herd animals. When they stampede out of one of their darlings, the result isn't a 5% decline. It is a vicious 20%-30% decline in a single day on massive volume. The stock will blast past the stop-loss orders without triggering them and the loss will be not 7.5%, but 20%-30%. Been there, done that.

The true godfather of momentum investing was Nicholas Darvas, a professional dancer who in 1961 wrote the runaway bestseller *How I made two Million Dollars in the Stock Market*. As Darvas relates in his book, he was given stock in a Canadian penny mining company in lieu of cash for a dancing performance. Two months later he checked to see how his stock was doing and was blown away to discover that it had almost quadrupled. He asked himself how long has this racket been going on. As I can fondly attest, it has been going on for a very long time indeed.

Penny mining stocks remain one of my favorite speculations because of their explosive potential. Darvas' book almost single handedly wiped out a generation of investors, myself among them. Darvas advocated a very high-risk policy of concentrating all of your firepower in as few as two or three highfliers, and then constantly increasing your position in these highfliers for as long as they went up. This was a very high-risk strategy that would either make you two million dollars very quickly, or send you to the poor house. I read his book in 1965 and for two horrific years I would only buy highfliers that had broken above their 52-week highs. It ended in disaster. Forget the instant self-gratification of momentum investing; it isn't worth it. At the end of the day, the stock market is a regression machine and not a momentum machine. It always regresses back to its mean.

TOUTED STOCKS

One of the things that have amazed me for more than 40 years as an investor is that only touted stocks are bought. In the absence of touting, stocks, even very good stocks, are ignored and not bought. We have all heard the saying that if something is too good to be true it probably isn't true. This is sound advice in investing with one important caveat. Investors have to know that the stock exists and of the merits of the stock. If they don't know that the stock exists, it can indeed be too good to be true until it is touted by the gurus and becomes "discovered".

As a small-cap investor, I am constantly telling my investment friends about new stocks that I have discovered. Unless they are familiar with the name, my friends will almost never consider purchasing these unknown stocks.

Over the years it has become clear to me that individual investors aren't even aware of this bias. This bias against untouted stocks results in individual investors mimicking the behavior of institutional investors. In short, they are overwhelmingly investors in the Nifty Fifty stocks that they see promoted on the financial news programs by their favorite guru. Another startling fact is the very low level of sophistication that one sees in these investors. This is contrary to what one hears about today's so-called "sophisticated investor". In their investing, they rely on blindly following the touts of their favorite guru to an extreme degree. When they do research it is always to check out a Nifty Fifty stock that a guru has recommended and never to buy some unknown small-cap stock that they have discovered.

The result of all this is the small-cap advantage. Everything else being equal, a small-cap or micro-cap stock will always sell at a discount to a big-cap stock of equal quality. They will also tend to sell at lower PE ratios and pay higher dividends than equivalent big-cap stocks.

Let's take an extreme example of this phenomenon. I could use one of my "cash cows" like Health Care Realty Trust, a REIT (real estate investment trust) that sells in the twenties and pays a 7% dividend. However, I like making my cases with a sledgehammer so I am going to select a penny stock that almost everyone would regard as being a worthless scam and prove to you that it is a value stock. I purchased this blue-chip penny mining stock at five cents a share. Now I know what you are thinking, how can a stock selling for five cents a share possibly be a value play? It is a Canadian stock that is listed on the TSX Venture Exchange. This is the old Vancouver stock exchange. The stock is Getty Copper. Its website is www.gettycopper.com. It has been incorporated since 1985 and has 32,743,000 shares outstanding. To the best of my knowledge it has never had a producing mine and has never earned a profit. Over the last 21 years, it has assembled the largest land package in the Highland Valley mining camp, with an amazing 115 square kilometers, that is 44 square miles of contiguous land claims. Getty's claims are located adjacent to the giant Highland Valley Copper mine, a consortium of three of the largest base metal producers in the business: Teck, Rio Algom, and Cominco. The Highland Valley mine has produced more than 460,000,000 pounds of copper up to now with a copper grade of .42%. This mining camp in its history has produced approximately eight billion pounds of copper with an average grade of .44% from nine major deposits. This is big game country. In 1992, Getty had an independent estimate done by Gower, Thompson and Associates to estimate the potential of its claims. They estimated 36 million tons of inferred but not proven copper reserves with a grade of .47% copper. Let's now examine Getty's recent ten-year annual high and low trading history. What do you think Pittsburgh Phil would say about a stock with a track record like this?

2004 .16 - .86		1999 .06 - .38
2003 .18 - .75		1998 .08 - .63
2002 .08 - .40		1997 .26 - 1.24
2001 .06 - .46		1996 .77 - 2.80
2000 .14 - .38		1995 .85 - 1.90

This is the kind of price action that has kept me investing in penny mining stocks for more than thirty years. Pittsburgh Phil would have said that Getty Copper has demonstrated a capacity to double, triple, and quadruple on an annual basis, and therefore has the potential to do so in the future. Let me add that this type of performance isn't unusual for low-priced stocks selling below $2.00 per share, as I will demonstrate later on. As a check, let's compare this performance with the bluest of the blue chips, General Electric. These prices have been adjusted for stock splits.

2005	$32.70 - 37.30	2000	$41.60 - 60.50
2004	$28.90 - 37.80	1999	$31.40 - 53.20
2003	$21.30 - 32.40	1998	$23.00 - 34.60
2002	$21.40 - 41.80	1997	$16.00 - 25.50
2001	$28.50 - 53.60	1996	$11.60 - 17.70

Pittsburgh Phil would inform us that General Electric has demonstrated an inability to double in any recent year and is therefore not likely to do so in the future. This is classic blue-chip performance. It is very, very rare for a blue chip to ever double in a year. How can they? It is only a slight exaggeration to claim that for a behemoth like GE to double, the market would have to dump a mountain of cash into GE that is the size of Mount Everest. For Getty, the only requirement would be for two or three speculators to invest $10,000 each on the same day, and Getty would go to the moon.

There are a few more important things to bring out about Getty. When it was selling for five cents a share, the market was valuing the whole corporation lock, stock, and barrel, not to mention its 44 square miles of land claims for a total price of $1,637,000 that is $37,204 for each square mile of land, not acre, but square mile. There is one more point of interest. The stock is very closely held by the CEO, John Lepinski, who owns 26% of the shares, this means that the float is only 24,223,000 shares. It would take very little positive news to send these shares to the moon. If tomorrow an investment analyst related just the facts that I have given you on CNBC News, $5.00 a share would be a possibility. That is the difference between a touted stock and a stock of which no one has ever heard. In the absence of a tout, even very good stocks can remain at "too good to be true" prices for years on end as I know only too well. At the time of writing, Getty's shares have risen to ten cents a share.

THE WAY IT USED TO BE

When I broke into investing more than forty years ago, fully rounded fundamental analysis as taught by Graham and Dodd was the norm. It was an analysis that gave great importance to things like dividends, book value, assets, and debt coverage ratios. While earnings were important, they weren't decisive. They were correctly understood to be highly variable and prone to fluctuate wildly with the business cycle. They weren't something that a prudent investor would rely on. The prudent investor relied on dividends because companies were very cautious about paying dividends that they couldn't comfortably afford to pay. Or as the wise old Wall Street adage has it "earnings are an opinion and cash is a fact" and dividends can only be paid out of cash.

As the years passed the growth schools championed a new orthodoxy that swept all before it. They stated that earnings were the sole determinate of stock market value, and that all other criteria such as dividends and book value were irrelevant. They regarded earnings as an independent variable that was magically suspended in space by a single gossamer thread, and that it was dependent on nothing else. And of course they were nuts. They attempted to reduce stock market investing to the following childish formula.

EARNINGS = STOCK MARKET VALUE

They were right to the extent that over the long run stock market value does closely track earnings. They were totally wrong, however, in trying to treat earnings as an independent variable. Earnings are a dependent variable. The correct formula is:

ASSETS DETERMINE EARNINGS AND EARNINGS DETERMINE VALUE.

The only way a company can earn a profit is through the deployment of its assets. A company's assets determine its earnings. Therefore, a company without assets can have no earnings. The interesting point here is that unlike earnings, which tend to bounce around like a ping-pong ball, assets tend to be tangible and easily identified. In my own investing I tend to avoid stocks that don't have tangible assets, such as advertising companies where the assets of the company go down in the elevator every night. A favorite category would be an oil driller. You will always know how many rigs the company has. You can also be sure that when all its rigs are operational, the company will gush cash and that if only 50% are operational, the company will gush red ink.

Another thing that has changed radically is the whole business of just what earnings are. It used to be easy. Until the 1980's there was only one type of earnings. Earnings were always trailing twelve-month GAAP earnings. GAAP stands for "generally accepted accounting principals", which is the only accounting standard accepted by the Securities and Exchange Commission. Anything else would have been regarded as a blatant fraud.

Today there are seven additional competing forms of earnings. And they are all highly suspect methods of analysis, or to be kinder, they are easier to manipulate. Here are all eight forms.

TRAILING GAAP EARNINGS
TRAILING OPERATING EARNINGS
TRAILING EBITDA EARNINGS
TRAILING PRO FORMA EARNINGS
ESTIMATED FUTURE GAAP EARNINGS
ESTIMATED FUTURE OPERATING EARNINGS
ESTIMATED FUTURE EBITDA EARNINGS
ESTIMATED FUTURE PRO FORMA EARNINGS

GAAP earnings require the subtraction of all expenses from income. Operating earnings don't subtract the so-called non-recurring or one-time expenses. Since these expenses aren't subtracted from income, the effect is to artificially increase a company's earnings. In one famous example a waste management company decided to hype its earnings by claiming that painting its garbage trucks were non-recurring expenses.

EBITDA stands for "earnings before interest, taxes, depreciation and amortization". You can of course make the case that depreciation and amortization are non-cash charges and are therefore real cash on hand, just like earnings. But interest and taxes are cash charges that must be paid.

The way pro forma earnings are used today is curious to say the least. It is supposed to mean a future estimate based on specific stated assumptions, but now it is even used on trailing reports. The thinking behind all of this is that if they told you the truth, you wouldn't buy their stock, so they will give you gibberish data that isn't usually regarded as being germane in an earnings report and release this data with great fanfare as if it were important, and you will be stupid enough to believe it and buy their stock. An example of this is an Internet company reporting that last quarter the number of hits they received rose 25%.

You will notice that the last four types of earnings are estimated future earnings. The problem with all attempts to estimate the future is that human beings are terrible at estimating the future. Reams of scientific studies have concluded that all attempts to estimate the future are in the long run no better than a coin toss. I regard all future earnings estimates with the total contempt that they so richly deserve. I would rather trust Madam Tussard the fortuneteller's estimates before I would trust any stock analyst's future estimates. By the way, Madam Tussard has a better record.

THE TYRANNY OF QUARTERLY EARNINGS

More needs to be said about earnings. Recently one of the TV financial talk shows was interviewing a highly regarded global mutual fund investor. He was asked what the major difference was between U.S. companies and foreign companies. He said the major difference was that American companies reported "ruler straight" earnings growth every year until they got into trouble, and then their stock would "blow up". While foreign companies earnings weren't "ruler straight" and would fluctuate with the business cycle and didn't have the same tendency to "blow up" when they didn't make their numbers.

I applauded. I think very few of the viewers realized what a damning indictment they had just heard on how Wall Street works. In the real world earnings fluctuate; they aren't "ruler-straight". The only way you get ruler-straight earnings is through what is commonly referred to as "earnings management". This is when you decide ahead of time what your earnings are going to be and then manage the books so that you come up with the right numbers. This is unethical, but if you know what you are doing, not illegal, at least not in the short run. Eventually, however, things get so bad that the ruler-straight earnings can only be obtained by fraud. As the post 2000 bear market has so painfully taught us.

It all started to go wrong in 1960's when Harold S. Geneen, the CEO of International Telephone & Telegraph, then a middle rung communications concern with operations primarily in Latin America, was transformed by this master accountant into a star Nifty Fifty conglomerate colossus with 350,000 employees in 80 countries. Geneen pioneered in the creative accounting that produced those wonderful ruler-straight earnings increases. During one heroic stretch, according to Fortune magazine, earnings grew for 58 consecutive quarters, an unheard of performance. Wall Street was agog. Under Geneen, earnings were ruler-straight. Until this point quarterly earnings weren't that important. People took the common sense view that 90 days was so short a period that any quarter's performance was essentially random and not significant. Not any more. Geneen taught Wall Street how to think stupid. Geneen understood something that is very basic. Most stock investors don't really want to own stocks at all, at least not real stocks that have fluctuating earnings. What they really want to own is stocks that act like high yielding CDs. They want high returns without the appearance of risk, and the way to give it to them is to report earnings increases that increase at the desired rate every quarter. No matter how great the insult to human intelligence, people would believe because they wanted to believe.

By the 1990's Wall Street gave people what they wanted to believe with a vengeance. The recent accounting scandals at multi-billion-dollar Goliath Fannie Mae are a classic example of this process. The company secretly squirreled away cookie jar reserves and then dipped into them as needed so they could deliver those "ruler-straight" earnings every quarter.

Alex Berenson has written a brilliant work about this called *The Number*, how the drive for quarterly earnings corrupted Wall Street and corporate America.

> On Wall Street, a place of little subtlety, earnings per share is known simply as "the number." As in "what was the number for Pfizer?" Earnings per share is the number for which all the other numbers are sacrificed. It is the distilled truth of a company's health. Earnings per share is the number that counts. Too bad it's a lie. Under the best of circumstances the figures in a quarterly report - earnings per share most of all - are approximations, best guesses based on a thousand other best guesses. Page xvi

> "The investment process consisted merely of finding prominent companies with a rising trend of earnings, and then buying their shares regardless of price. Hence the sound policy was to buy only what everyone else was buying," Ben Graham had written of investment trusts in 1934. Not much has changed. Looking back on the 1990's from 2002, one fund manger would write that, "what has taken the place of detailed fundamental analysis over the years is the wholesale adoption of earnings per share as the sole basis for security analysis." Page 165

BUY LOW. SELL HIGH.

Everyone has heard the above trite statement. The important point about the above statement is that only a small minority of investors ever follows it. The overwhelming majority of all investors, if given the opportunity between buying a stock that has increased in value 300% in the last two years or a stock that has fallen in value 80% in the last two years, will always pick the stock that is up 300%. When stocks are on the bargain counter, investors flee in panic, but when stocks are selling at record highs, investors are lined up three times around the block to buy them. When put to the test, people don't believe in "buy low, sell high". What people believe in is the greater fool theory, and in the fullness of time they all become the greater fool. What is surprising is that people are totally unaware of this bias. It has been said that the last thing that a fish ever sees is the water that surrounds it. I have been watching this bias carefully for 40 years. When I told friends about some contrarian play that I had discovered that had fallen say 80% in value, they would recoil in horror and would invariably buy some highflier selling at some obscene price that left no margin for error. It is almost comical to see their stunned disbelief when these stocks blow up.

DANCING SLICK

In this world it is our unchallenged assumptions that kill us. Assumptions that we take so much for granted that it never enters our head to question them. In the stock market these unchallenged assumptions are particularly deadly.

The deadliest of them all is the dancing slick assumption. It is almost a universal assumption among all new investors, and most old timers for that matter, that the way to make money in the stock market is by dancing slickly into and out of stocks gathering a quick 15%-20% in each dance. The problem with this is that when you research stocks, you find the best stocks first and after selling them for your quick 15% profit, you find yourself replacing them with inferior prospects. What ends up happening is that the stocks that you sell for your 15% profit keep going up after you sell them and your inferior replacements can't get out of their own way. The truth is that the number of great stocks selling at bargain prices is always limited in this world; and when you find one, you have to keep it and ride it for all that it is worth.

Super investor Warren Buffet is the ultimate proof of this. He is frequently quoted as saying that his favorite holding period is forever. It is disturbing to analyze the stocks that made him the world's second richest man. There isn't one highflying wonder stock in the whole group. Just sound stocks purchased at bargain prices. Armies of investors have bought and sold these same stocks for trivial profits. The only thing that separated these investors from Warren Buffet type returns is that he bought and held, whereas they bought and sold. On Wall Street, patience is the most rewarded virtue.

JESSE LIVERMORE AND THE CASINO THESIS

Much more needs to be said about this matter. Investors today live in a world dominated by the fraudulent thesis of the momentum school. As I have already indicated, they bestride the investment world like a colossus sweeping all before them and leaving behind them the fearful carnage of an ever-growing army of broken and shattered investors who believed that stampeding with the herd was a profitable endeavor. What is even more astounding is that their ideology doesn't work, or to be more accurate, it only works over the short term.

The mechanics of the stock market insure that every momentum investor can have a hot hand and coin money for two or three years. However, that happy period of delusion will be replaced by a grim eternity in which the hitherto magical system stops working. As I have been at pains to explain, the Graham & Dodd School of fundamental analysis, as championed by super investor Warren Buffet, can document their superiority over the momentum thesis. If you ask who is the Warren Buffet of momentum investing, the answer is that there is no one. There are no momentum investors who can come within light years of achieving his documented performance over a period of decades. To find a challenger, you have to go back to the 1920's, the heyday of the great Jesse Livermore, who is still regarded as perhaps the greatest speculator and momentum player of all time. The book which Jesse is credited with ghostwriting is the classic, *Reminiscences Of A Stock Operator*, by Edwin Lefevre, which was written in 1923 and which is still in print, and to this day is regarded as a stock market classic by worshipful momentum players.

The great Jesse Livermore was born in 1877. He started his career by making a killing in every type of stock and commodity in a special type of brokerage firm that is outlawed today, but at that time were called "bucket shops" and are too complicated to explain in this work. After he left the bucket shops behind him, he made his first fortune in 1906 by shorting the Union Pacific railroad, which had been severely damaged by the San Francisco earthquake, and became famous as the boy plunger of Wall Street. Despite his great talent, he declared bankruptcy four times in his long career. After each bankruptcy, fellow investors would grub stake him for his new assault on the markets. His greatest triumph was in 1929 when his bear market raids, in the minds of many, broke the stock market and made him a fortune of $100 million, a staggering sum in those days. But after that, it was all downhill. In 1940 his once great fortune gone and facing a fifth bankruptcy, he blew his brains out in an exclusive New York nightclub. In his suicide letter he stated that his life had been a failure and that he no longer knew what worked. Since his death no momentum player or trend chaser has arrived to pick up his mantle because the momentum thesis in the long run takes back from you all that it has given you, and more.

Let's carefully analyze what is wrong with this school. It believes that the stock market is a casino, and that stocks are lottery tickets with no intrinsic value. The stock market is always right. If it says today that a stock is worth $5 and tomorrow that the same stock is worth $50 in the absence of any valid reason, then the stock market has been right both days. Any opinion about stocks is wrong headed because your opinion may deviate from that of the stock market, and where would you be then? There is, however, one opinion that you must have and that is the stock's trend or direction. You are above all else a "trend chaser". You buy what is going up and you sell what is going down. Their last fatal error is that they think in terms of days or weeks, when you must think in terms of years.

The Graham & Dodd School believes that the stock market is an investor's cathedral and not a casino, and that stocks are ownership certificates and not lottery tickets. This school understands that if you treat the stock market as a casino, then it will treat you as a gambler. It understands that the stock market isn't perfect and that market price and intrinsic value can deviate greatly, and when it does, your profit potential is maximized. It recognizes that the greatest profits and the surest profits can only be made by long-term investing. Patience is the most rewarded investment virtue. Lastly, because stocks fluctuate greatly in the long term, you must be willing to hold on to your stocks even if they go down. By definition you can't be a long-term investor if you sell your stocks as soon as they go down because they will always go down, but they won't stay down. Therefore your success as an investor will be determined by your willingness to hold your stocks when they do go down, as they inevitably will.

It is critical that you don't regard your stocks as a scraps of paper, an intangible asset that gives you ownership over nothing but a line in the stock tables that tells you volume and price and nothing else. If you believe that the only thing that you own is a line on the stock pages that is bouncing up and down every day like a ping-pong ball for no discernible reason, then why wouldn't you sell it if it begins to go down? After all, for all you know, it could go down forever. Above all else you must be aware of the fact that you own a real live company with real live assets, and not just a lottery ticket.

I insist on thinking of myself as a captain of industry. I own millions of acres of timberlands and railroads. My ships plow the high seas. I own oil wells and oil drillers and oil pipelines and refineries. I own gold mines and silver mines and copper, lead, zinc, coal, and uranium mines. I own shopping malls and office buildings. It is only when you understand that you own assets of real intrinsic value, which you purchased at bargain prices, that you will be able to hold on to them when the market turns against you, and it will turn against you. But it won't stay against you.

HUNTING TIGERS IN INDIA

On July 1, 1948 two shrewd investors purchased the same stock at the same price and for the same reason. Both had carefully analyzed the stock and concluded that it was a great bargain. The next day one of the investors departed by cruise ship for a long-delayed tiger hunting expedition in India. While this great white hunter was bagging tigers in India, his stock purchase underwent a vicious 30% decline. The reason for the decline has been lost in the mists of time, but some people say it was because an alleged stock analyst had issued a negative report on the stock. The investor who had remained in New York panicked and sold his stock at a 30% loss. Naturally he managed to sell the stock at almost its exact bottom. Meanwhile, the great white hunter in India knew nothing about this; he was having a ball blazing away at tigers. He was using a machine gun (in those days they paid a bounty on tigers). The bounty on tigers was so much more profitable when you were using a machine gun. More than three months later, the great white hunter and his tiger skins returned to New York, and he discovered that his stock by this time had reversed and was now up 30%.

Contemplate this well, the only distinction between these two shrewd investors is that one sold because he knew that he had a loss and the other didn't sell because he didn't know that he had a loss. The point of this fable is that selling stocks that you believe in is a fool's game.

The almost universal law that is taught on Wall Street is to cut your losses quickly, after all, how many 10% losses can you take? The correct answer is that stocks fluctuate and if you hold on to the stock, your 10% loss will in time turn into a profit. What must be understood is that corrections in the 15% to 30% range are normal in the stock market and aren't some horrific holocaust that must be avoided by dumping the stock in a panic. If you sell stocks that you have researched and believe in for no other reason than that they are going down, then you can't beat this game. Corrections are normal; they are the stock market's way of testing your faith in your own judgment. The market will try to convince you that you are wrong when you aren't wrong. This is the market's supreme test, which all investors are subjected to. Research your stock investments and stick to your guns when they go down, and they will go down, but they won't stay down. This is how markets work. If you can do this, you will have met the stock market's supreme test and your success is assured because all the other stock market tests are child's play in comparison to this brutal test. If you have no faith in your own judgment, then the stock market is going to be a vale of tears for you. You will constantly be blown out of stocks that you were right about and suffer losses on stocks that six months after you have sold them are solidly in the profit column.

In the end, what all investors have to deal with is the hard hand of the stock market. The secret of investment success is to buy stocks at bargain prices and to sell them when they have become overpriced. This is doable. What isn't doable is to ascertain the price action of your investment in between these two points. The brutal reality is that the space between these two points will always be what the ancient mapmakers called "terra incognito" (unknown lands), and to the investor they will always be unknown lands because no accurate map exists of the rocks and shoals that will destroy your financial ship, and no accurate map can ever be drawn of these treacherous rocks and shoals because the daily price action of stocks is determined not by rational investors, but by mobs of hysterical day traders and momentum players whose time horizon is usually measured in minutes. There is no rational basis for forecasting these short-term trends because in the market, all short-term trends are random; and it is becoming more random and violent all the time. As the army of true believers, people who actually research the stocks that they buy and, what is far more important, believe in these stocks and their intrinsic worth, keeps shrinking, the army of the "know nothings" whose only belief is in "trend chasing" keeps growing.

I have just finished reading an Internet report on average investor-holding periods for NYSE stocks. In 1940 the typical investor-holding period was almost ten years. In the 1950's and the 1960's it fluctuated at around seven or eight years. By 1975 it had fallen to five years. Today it is 11 months. While the average investor probably has slightly above average intelligence as a collective, he is as dumb as a fence post; unless the fence post is having a bad day. Today the average investor believes that the stock market is a casino and that he has purchased a lottery ticket. As a result he parks his brain at the door when he enters the casino and stumbles around with the rest of the sheep, the goats, and the cattle while waiting to participate in the next tout inspired stampede. The type of news that 30 or 40 years ago would have been regarded as being so inconsequential as to hardly register in the market will now send the market skyrocketing or spiraling into the depths. It is becoming harder and harder every year to find rationally priced stocks. What is becoming more and more common is a two-tier market. One tier of crushed stocks that the "trend chasers" have chased into the gutter and that are selling at prices that are too cheap to believe, and a second tier that the "trend chasers" have chased into orbit and are selling at prices that are too high to believe.

In a world in which most investors are clueless to the very notion of a stock having an intrinsic value, let alone knowing how to analyze intrinsic value, the value player is king. If you would but stay the course and resist the futile temptation of trying to predict daily price action. The most dangerous delusion of all is the delusion that when your investment starts falling in value, there is some rational method of selling before it declines even further in value and then by using some magical technique that doesn't exist predict the bottom and then buy back your investment. What a joke that is! Generations of investors have been sent to their doom by believing this idiotic delusion. This delusion will only ruin you. Only Madame Tussard, the fortuneteller, can do that, and I have lost her phone number.

INEFFICIENT MARKETS

Markets vary greatly in their efficiency. The more efficient a market is, the lower its volatility. The more inefficient a market is, the higher its volatility. Volatility is defined as the spread between a stock's high and low in any 52-week period. Think of the stock market as a pyramid. At the top of the pyramid are the Nifty Fifty stocks. These stocks have the lowest volatility. The reason they have the lowest volatility is that these stocks are watched like a hawk by thousands of stock analysts. As a result of this intense laser-like concentration, these stocks never stray too far from their intrinsic market value. Below them is the S&P 5OO Stock Index, which have a somewhat higher volatility because they aren't exposed to as much analyst scrutiny. As we descend down the pyramid, the stocks at each level receive less and less analytical attention. And as we descend, the stocks at each level have a greater propensity to stray from intrinsic value. The volatility at each level steadily increases. As the volatility increases, the probability of making huge profits and loses also increases because the probability grows that the market won't be appraising these stocks accurately. At the bottom rungs of the pyramid is a magic area, the area of the sub five-dollar-a-share stock. It is common for stocks in this price range to not be followed by a single analyst. But it gets better, these stocks are almost never purchased by institutional investors because these stocks lack the size and liquidity that institutions require. In addition, stocks selling for less than $5.00 a share aren't marginable. This casts a pall over these low-priced stocks and they are regarded as being too risky. Thus, these stocks are followed by no one and are purchased by no one. Well by now you have probably figured out that this isn't exactly true.

In 1988 it was my good fortune to receive a report, which I still have, that had been done by Yorkton Securities, a well-regarded Canadian brokerage firm. The implications in the report are dynamite. The report concerns itself with stock market volatility. The report stated that over the last 65 years the average volatility of the S&P 500 is 35%, but the average volatility for stocks selling for less than a dollar was a staggering 265%. I felt like I had struck gold. It was confirmation of what I had suspected for years.

Another seldom-considered advantage is the enormous leverage inherent in low-priced stocks. If I invest $1,000 in a stock selling for $1.00 a share and the stock goes up $1.00, I have doubled my money. I have made $1,000. If I had invested that $1,000 in a company selling for $50.00 a share and it had gone up $1.00 a share, I would have made a profit of only $20.00. It is amazing how seldom this critical factor is considered by investors. What more do you need to know?

In my own investing I don't like to buy stocks that sell for more than $20.00 a share and I refuse to pay more than $40.00 a share for any stock. When I discover a stock that is selling above $40.00 a share that is too attractive to turn down, I will buy a two year leap option on the stock which enables me to control 100 shares of the stock for a fraction of its selling price.

CONVERSATIONS

Since investing in stocks is such a big part of my life, I am constantly getting into conversations with my friends about stocks. As I have already stated, it was these frustrating conversations that led me to want to write about my experiences in the stock market. I have a story to tell. A story about a stock universe that almost no one even knows exists. I don't know anybody who invests in the small-cap and micro-cap unknowns that I invest in. Everybody I know invests only in Nifty-Fifty stocks.

Not so long ago I was attending a real-estate seminar in a Wyndham hotel in Miami. As I was chatting with a friend I brought up the fact that I was glad they were holding the seminar at the hotel as I had just purchased stock in Wyndham. Everything was going fine until I made the mistake of telling him what I had paid for the stock, 70 cents a share. As soon as he heard this he started gawking at me as if I had just grown three heads. This isn't an unusual experience. It was all downhill from there. I tried to explain to him that Wyndham could be a classic turnaround situation. This was a stock that owned thousands of hotel rooms throughout the country. It had gotten into trouble by expanding too rapidly and taking on too much debt, which it couldn't repay. But this was an asset-rich stock that in my opinion could sell off enough of its hotels to pay off its debts. Another strong possibility was a buyout offer from another hotel chain. He was having none of it. I wasn't surprised; I have been having conversations like this for many years. In the end, Wyndham was sold out to another hotel chain for the disappointing price of $1.15 a share. The chain has decided to retain the Wyndham name.

Here are some typical comments I have heard over the years.

"Tell me Fred what do you invest in? Did you say short-line railroads? I thought they only existed on a Monopoly board." "Did you say coal mines another dying 19th century industry?" "Did you say uranium stocks? My grandfather has a ton of worthless uranium stocks in the attic that he purchased in the 1950's." "Did you say penny-mining stocks? You must be stupid! Don't you know that all penny-mining stocks are scams that are operated by crooks?" "I would like to hear more about your weirdo investments, Fred but I have urgent business in Outer Mongolia. I will give you a call when I get back."

Standard & Poor's most important product is its justly famous one-page stock reports that are found in loose ring binders in libraries and brokers offices throughout the country. About two thirds of the way down the page you will find a one-line statement that tells you what the value of $10,000 made in this company five years ago would be worth today. As of the day, this is being written $10,000 invested in Microsoft five years ago would be worth $7,921, and $10,000 invested in Intel would be worth a whopping $5,953. Not exactly the road to the Promised Land, is it? Unless of course the promised land you are going to is hell. Now you know why you can't get rich investing in Nifty-Fifty stocks. Even high-tech champions like Microsoft and Intel.

Now let me compare this performance with two short-line railroads that I am keen on. The value of $10,000 invested in Rail America five years ago would be worth $11,801 today, and $10,000 invested in the Providence & Worcester railroad would be worth $21,322 today. That is right; two rinky-dink 19th century railroads outperformed two of the mightiest high-tech giants of our age. Let's take a look at coal, that other dying 19th century industry. The value of $10,000 invested five years ago in coal producer Consolidated Energy would be worth $25,322 today. Welcome to my world.

However, what really bothers me is that I have been investing in penny mining stocks for decades and, fool that I am, I totally missed the fact that they are all scams and run by crooks. How could I have missed this fact? How could I have gone so wrong? Let's see, could it be the bushel basket of penny mining stocks that I have owned that have gone up more than 100%? Could it be the dozen or so stocks that have gone up more than 500%? Could it be the five stocks that have gone up more than 1,000%? That is it. That is the answer.

SUPERIOR INVESTMENTS

I will of course invest in anything and everything that I believe is selling at a bargain price. But by now the astute reader will have realized that Nifty-Fifty and S&P 500 stocks aren't on the menu. Having said that, over the years I have specialized in inefficient markets, those obscure out of the mainstream and out of favor investment sectors that the Wall Street touts barely even know exist. In short I am a contrarian value investor because that is what works. What works is buying stocks that are in the gutter. Stocks that have been crushed pulverized and left for dead, stocks that have lost 80%-90% of their value. What doesn't work is the ever-popular stampeding with the herd, which is forever chasing the latest highflier. When you stampede with the cattle, the sheep, and the goats the best you can hope to do is average, and you can easily do far worse than average as I can attest. I have vivid memories of my career as a herd animal and most of them are ugly. Wall Street has many canyons and my fellow herd animals and I have stampeded off all of them. The falls can be brutal and I have the scars to prove it. Below are my favorite investments.

JUNK BOND MUTUAL FUNDS
EMERGING MARKET BOND MUTUAL FUNDS
CONVERTIBLE BONDS
INDIVIDUAL JUNK BONDS
REITS (REAL ESTATE INVESTMENT TRUSTS)
OIL & GAS ROYALTY TRUSTS
CANADIAN INCOME TRUSTS
MLPS (MASTER LIMITED PARTNERSHIPS)
SUB $5.00 STOCKS
PENNY MINING STOCKS
TWO-YEAR OPTION LEAPS

The astute reader will notice an interesting fact. The top eight categories are all income plays. Only the bottom three are non-income plays. It is time to consider the importance of income.

SPECULATING AND INVESTING

We all use the terms speculating and investing interchangeably, but there is a critical difference between the two terms. For many years I was aware of the difference, but I regarded it as a difference without a distinction. It took me about 20 years to understand the critical importance between the two terms and its massive impact on investment success.

A speculation is an investment that pays no income. The only way you can earn a profit on a speculation is for the investment to rise in value. An investment, however, can earn a profit without rising in value. It has an income stream. It pays dividends or interest; and implicit in this is the assumption that the income stream to a greater or lesser extent supports the value of the investment.

For 20 years I couldn't have cared less about this distinction. I wanted to get rich quick and I knew that dividends weren't going to get me there. As a result I went out of my way to avoid dividend-paying stocks. But as the years progressed I was confronted with the ugly fact that my speculations weren't getting the job done. The truth was my speculations were struggling to equal the riskless return I could have gotten from a savings account. By this time I knew tons of stocks that paid more in dividends than a savings account paid in interest, and I could get the capital gains for free. Adding income plays to my stock portfolio was one of the wisest decisions of my life and is an absolute must for long-term investment success. Without income investments, you will find yourself on an eternal treadmill to nowhere. You will find it difficult, if not impossible, to put two winning years back to back. Been there, done that. The following table indicates how many years it would take an investment to double at the stated rate of interest.

THE POWER OF COMPOUNDING

1% = 72 years	9% = 8 years
2% = 36 years	10% = 7 years
3% = 24 years	11% = 6.5 years
4% = 18 years	12% = 6 years
5% = 14 years	13% = 5.5 years
6% = 12 years	14% = 5 years
7% = 10 years	15% = 4.8 years
8% = 9 years	16% = 4.5 years

There it is, the key to the kingdom! Compounding is the royal road to wealth. It is impossible to look at these tables and not be impressed with what they are indicating. When the power of compounding is coupled with dollar cost averaging, you have a weapon in your financial arsenal that is without peer. Dollar cost averaging is the automatic reinvesting of interest or dividends back into your investment as soon as they have been earned. The magic of dollar cost averaging is that by mathematical law over any sustained holding period, your cost of acquiring additional shares must be less than the average cost of the stock during the holding period. That is because you will automatically be acquiring fewer new shares of stock when the price is high and more shares of stock when the price is low over the holding period. When dollar cost averaging is coupled with a high dividend paying junk bond fund, REIT or Royalty Company for five or more years, the result is eye popping. When you own such an investment and the share price takes a heavy hit, rejoice because your profits will be greatly magnified when the stock recovers. Indeed in a stock that fluctuates enough, dollar cost averaging can reduce the number of years required for the stock to double by two or more years; and far more than that if the dividend or interest rate is low enough to allow many years for the stock to double.

I can't leave this issue here. It is way too important. After you have been a market player for a few years, it is impossible to ignore how stupid the stock market has become. A classic example of this mind-blowing stupidity is that it dumps high dividend paying stocks which have secure covered dividends in the same manner and to the same degree that it dumps stocks that pay no dividend whatsoever. This is truly crazy and yet you will see it happen again and again.

Let's take a classic example. A REIT that is selling for $10 and is paying a secure 8% dividend. That is until some prestigious stock analyst announces that in his opinion REIT earnings have peaked and will probably fall. Wall Street will treat this stock exactly the way it will treat a stock that pays no dividend; it can easily drop this stock 20%. What do we now have? Prior to this insanity we had a $10 stock that paid an 8% dividend and therefore would double if we reinvested the dividends in a DRIP (dividend reinvestment program), which is what we should always do. The stock in a DRIP plan would double in nine years. We now have an $8 stock with an 80-cent dividend that is now yielding 10% and will double in seven years. When you stop to think about it, that isn't a bad trade off.

Let's assume the market really went nuts and dropped the stock 30%. After all, it is Wall Street lore that all declining stocks must be sold immediately before they fall to zero. After all, we know that all falling stocks are destined to fall to zero, don't we? Our $10 stock has now fallen to $7 and therefore is paying a yield of 11%. At 11% the stock will double in about 6.5 years. Not exactly the end of the world is it? Of course in the real world none of this will happen. Within a year or two at the most the stock market will recover from its insanity and realize that 10% or 11% is way to generous a dividend for commercial real estate which has a proven habit of raising its rentals on a regular basis. Watch out for this, it is as close to being a sure thing as Wall Street offers. I make it a habit to always increase my position in a stock when this happens to stocks that I own.

THE KOGER EQUITY CRISIS

In my 28th year as an investor I made the most important investment of my life; in Koger Equity, an office REIT that I was very keen on. The REIT had developed debt repayment problems and it was forced to eliminate its dividend. The stock dropped like a rock from about $20 a share to $9¾ where I pounced on it like a hawk. At that price Koger Equity was according to my analysis an incredible value. Because it was such a screaming bargain, I decided to make a huge bet on the stock; I think it was about 25%-30% of my investment capital.

Unfortunately for me, Wall Street didn't share my conviction that Koger Equity was an incredible value. I watched in stunned disbelief as the stock fell and fell and fell. As the stock fell, I realized that there could only be one explanation for a stock with so much value to be going into a death spiral. The company didn't have a mere debt repayment problem as I had thought, it was going bankrupt and I had been too stupid to realize it. In a panic I sold the stock at $3 3/8th before it went to zero. I was devastated, crushed. Not only had I taken the most horrific financial loss of my life, but also it was now clear to me that I would have to find a new profession. It was only a matter of time before the state of Florida discovered that it had licensed a commercial real estate appraiser who wasn't only stupid, but incompetent as well and demand that I turn in my license.

I of course managed to sell Koger Equity at almost its exact bottom. The exact bottom for the stock was $3 1/8th. I then watched shell-shocked as the stock began its relentless rise, $4.00 a share, $5.00 a share, $6.00 a share, $7.00 a share. Finally I bought back the stock at $7½ my only intelligent decision in the whole fiasco. I was suicidal. I was ready to fly to New York City so I could hurl myself off of the Empire State Building and end my wretched life.

There is nothing more painful than to lose money on a stock that you are right about. Yet it is one of the most common of all Wall Street experiences. The technical Wall Street term for this is being whipsawed. I had been whipsawed many times in my investment career, but this was the final blow. I have always been able to pick winners and I have the records to prove it over hundreds of transactions. But the ugly truth of the matter was that being whipsawed was killing me. I should have been a highly successful investor; instead I was barely successful. My Koger Equity loss guaranteed that I would have another losing year.

As I reviewed my records, I faced the bitter realization that I would have made more money if I had placed my capital in a savings account. All those thousands of hours spent in the library researching investments, and I do mean thousands of hours. All those years of subscribing to Barron's, Forbes, and the Northern Miner, not to mention the forty or so books I had read on investing. It had to be at least that many. It had all been in vain. I was facing a crisis that I couldn't resolve, an enigma that had been haunting me right from the beginning.

I had been trained as an economist and my profession was real estate appraiser. Everything that I had been taught and believed in stated that the decisions of the market place were superior to that of any individual or subgroup because the markets represented the total sum of all human knowledge on the subject. And yet after 28 years, I had abundant proof that this was false. Time and time again I would take a position in a stock. If the stock declined 5% or 10%, I would hold on and see what happened. If it dropped 15% or 20% I would sell my position. The voice of God had spoken and who was I to argue with the market? Who was I to argue with God? I would then watch in disbelief as the stock reversed course and then begin its relentless march upward past my purchase price. There I would be the ultimate bag holder holding another loss on a stock that I had been right on from the beginning. The evidence was after 28 years that I should trust my own judgment and not allow myself to be blown out of my stocks. However, I had no confidence in my judgment when it conflicted with the market. What about the insiders? What about the stock analysts? What about all those people who had superior knowledge about that particular stock? I was at my wit's end. I simply couldn't resolve this problem. I didn't know what to do.

Then it hit me, I had my eureka moment. I realized for the very first time that the stock market wasn't a market at all. They call it a market, but it isn't a market at all, at least not in the short-term. In the long-term it does indeed oscillate around market value. But in the short-term it is nothing more than a random action machine. As herds of so-called investors mindlessly stampede hither and yon driven by fear and greed based on the latest tout or news report. Here is an official definition of market value that is used by real estate appraisers:

> The most probable price as of a specific date in cash or in terms equivalent to cash for which the specified property should sell after reasonable exposure in a competitive market under all conditions requisite to a fair sale, with buyer and seller acting prudently, knowledgeably, and for self interest and assuming that neither is under duress.

Today, the stock market fails the above test in two ways. First it is dominated by armies of day traders and momentum players who aren't acting knowledgeably. They have no independent opinion whatsoever as to the worth of the stocks that they are buying and selling. Indeed they would correctly regard having an opinion on the market value of the stocks that they are trading as dangerous. After all, it might conflict with that of the market. And just where would they be then? They are forever chasing the latest trend. In no sense are these armies of buyers and sellers making independent, knowledgeable decisions about the market; which is what a market value requires.

The second way the stock market fails the above test is the question of duress. Fear and greed are everywhere. In any given day it could be argued the majority of the buyers and sellers are operating under duress, often under severe distress. Therefore the stock market fails the requirements of a market in the short-term, but not the long-term. The realization that I wasn't competing against a market freed me. I knew I couldn't compete against a market, but I had every confidence that I could compete against a herd of cattle. For the first time I could trust my judgment and stand by my stock picks with confidence when the market turned against me. The results were dramatic. My loser years were over.

Today I use a barbell strategy to allocate my investment capital. This means that I allocate capital on the extremes; two thirds of my capital is allocated to income plays that pay a dividend or interest of at least 6%. Before the bear market of 2000 I could get at least 8% on all of my income plays, but then the market discovered REITs and today it is almost impossible to get more than 6% on an REIT. The other third is allocated to speculations that don't pay a dividend. Because I am a riverboat gambler at heart, I insist on massive diversification to protect me. I won't invest more than 5% of my investment capital in any position, and this is unusual. The truth is I have reached the point in my investment career where 5% of my capital is more than I feel comfortable with placing in any single position. My typical position is about 2% of my investment capital. In my micro bets, which is what I call my investments in the sub $5.00 stocks, I use about 1% of my investment capital and in penny stocks my typical investment is a quarter of 1% to half of 1% of my investment capital. This enables me to pick up the iron dice of destiny and throw them again and again and again. In a very real sense, I am using loaded dice and the more I throw them the more I win. That is why I currently have about 147 positions in my portfolio. The riverboat gambler's most intriguing insight on the stock market is that all investors use loaded dice if they only knew it. What I mean by this is that when you invest in the market, the odds are with you.

Since 1926 the stock market has averaged a return of about 10% a year. The market over any protracted period has an upward bias. We have all heard about those experiments with chimps that throw darts at a stock page and get superior performance, they are all true and if humans threw the darts, the results would be the same. In another words if you just pick stocks using any random method, you have better than a 50% chance of winning. And if you use research to pick bargains, it goes higher. Over a 40-year period I have been right over 60% of the time with my speculations and about 80% of the time with my lower risk income plays. As Richard Russell writer of the justly famous Dow Theory Letters once said in a Barron's article: "Nobody is right in this business more than 80% of the time." Yet most investors do much worse than the facts indicate they should.

I have just finished reading a report called the "Dalbar Studies". This study compares the performance of mutual funds versus what the average investor in these mutual funds made. These studies always discover the same thing. They discover that by some strange miracle these investors always do much worse than the stocks or mutual funds in which they are invested. Of course there is no miracle involved in this inferior performance, there is only the usual "herd mentality". The study contrasts the average 12.22% annual gain of the S&P 500 between 1984-2002, and the unbelievably pathetic average return of only 2.57% during the same period by investors. And bond investors were no smarter, the government bond index gained 11.7% on average, but the average investor in these bonds received only 4.2% on average. The reason for this appallingly bad performance is always the same. The wise investor researches his investment and invests based on this research. The fool will have none of this. The fool's only interest is in stampeding with the herd. After all, how can every Tom, Dick, and Harry be wrong? The fool is always chasing, chasing, chasing. Chasing hot tips and chasing performance after it has already occurred is a formula that will put you in the poor house.

I stated earlier that in this world it is our unchallenged assumptions that kill us. One of the most deadly of these assumptions is that the key to investment success is to cut your losses quickly; as the massive army of Wall Street never tires of telling us the trend is your friend. There is no reason to buy or hold a stock that isn't going up in value and you must immediately sell any stock that is going down in value or you will be destroyed. For many years I believed so completely in this assumption that I thought it should be carved in granite on the sides of mountains. As I write this I can just see this being read by an enraged momentum player. The core doctrine of momentum investing is that you must sell you losers quickly before they go to zero. After all, declining stocks are headed to zero, aren't they? I can just see the smoke coming out of his ears before the committed momentum player does a triple somersault and bounces on his head three times as he reads this heresy.

I have a question for the reader, if the stock market has a perpetual upward bias over any prolonged period and if everyone including chimps throwing darts at a stock table has better than a 50/50 chance of winning, what is the only thing that can destroy you as an investor? The answer is selling your positions at a loss. Think about it. It was selling my losing positions that almost killed me for 28 years. Since we know that no one can be right more than 80% of the time, we must have the safety net of diversification to save us from our inevitable mistakes. No more than 5% on a standard investment and no more than 1% on my low-priced riverboat gambles is a model that has served me well.

Speaking of riverboat gambles, it is time to consider penny mining stocks, as they are my favorite investment category. No other category is capable of delivering the explosive profits that penny mining stocks can on a chump change investment.

Today's riverboat gamblers don't hang out in a casino. They hang out in the stock exchanges of Toronto and Vancouver. Stick around and I will show you how to join the club. You can become like us. Cool and calculating, with ice water in your veins and with nerves of steel. You can buy one of those wonderful southern plantation hats that the riverboat gamblers used to wear and you can hang out at riverboat casinos like the Mississippi Belle. You can tell people that you do your serious gambling on the stock market because the odds are so much better. It will be an exiting adventure. It will be wonderful.

Now I know what you are thinking. You are thinking: "No way, Jose! I don't have a drop of ice water in my veins and I don't have nerves of steel. I am not going to invest in some scary penny mining stock or some unknown stock that I have never heard of. I work too hard for my money."

It is precisely this fear that paralyzes investors and prevents them from having the success they deserve. The way it works is like this. People say to themselves: high risk = high rewards. And I'm not willing to take the high risks that will earn me the high rewards, so that cancels the equation. The true secret of the riverboat gambler is that he realizes that he must bet small and bet repeatedly. Each loss is insignificant and the rewards are huge in relation to the losses. As I have said, we are all using loaded dice and don't know it. The barbell strategy is an excellent template for your exciting new career. The Mississippi Belle is in reach.

By the way, fellow riverboat gamblers, I thought you would like to know that the Mississippi Belle is located in Vicksburg, Mississippi, my brother Ray and I spent some time on the Mississippi belle when we were visiting the famous Civil War battlefield at Vicksburg. I am a Civil War buff.

PENNY MINING STOCKS

Picture this; the year is 1968, the place is the USS Little Rock, the flagship of the mighty U.S. sixth fleet. We were sailing in the Mediterranean Sea off the west coast of Italy somewhere between Rome and Naples. I was waiting to go on watch in the CIC (the Combat Information Center) or as we fondly call it: the center of intense confusion. I was reading a magazine article; I think it was Saga magazine that had my undivided attention. The article was written by someone who had just made a killing speculating in penny mining stocks. I have always been fascinated with the concept of making big bucks on a chump change investment and this was right up my alley. The most important part of this article was that the writer informed the reader that if you were going to speculate in penny mining stocks, you had to subscribe to the Northern Miner, and what is even more important, he gave the address. I sent off a letter requesting a subscription. I remain a subscriber to this day.

Now I know what you are thinking. You are thinking; why penny mining stocks? Why not penny stocks in general? What is so great about penny mining stocks?

I thought you would never ask. First, it needs to be understood that I only invest in mining stocks that are listed on the Toronto stock exchange or its related junior stock exchange the TSE Venture exchange. Contrary to popular belief, our northern friends do an excellent job of policing and regulating their mining industry so long as perfection isn't expected. And they provide an excellent filter by mandating minimum requirements that the companies must adhere to. How many penny stocks do you know of that are listed on an exchange and have to meet minimum requirements that aren't mining related? The correct answer is almost none. Another advantage is that only a tiny percentage of these stocks are producers. The vast majority of these stocks have no operating income at all. I regard this as a plus because then they can be analyzed strictly as an asset play; and they are asset plays with a vengeance. There is no other investment on earth that routinely has such colossal asset values in relation to their stock prices. Then there is their astounding ability which no other type of stock possesses to go into hibernation for years, if necessary for decades, and maintain their listing. All other stocks perish if they can't maintain operations. Lastly I am of the belief that we are entering a golden age of natural resources that should last for at least another decade. I have already given you the example of Getty Copper.

Let's take a look at Moneta Porcupine mines. It was incorporated in 1910, and I believe it has been listed on the TSE since 1926. It was a gold producer from 1938-1943, but since then it has produced nothing. It owns ten gold properties on which there are a total of 26 past producing mines. It has 1679 mining claims. Each mining claim is 40 acres, for a total 67,160 acres. The stock currently sells for about 16 cents a share. At that price the entire market capitalization is about $11,860,000. That is for the whole company, lock, stock, and barrel; not to mention the 67,160 acres! At that price the market is placing a value of

$176.59 for every acre that Moneta owns. Of course Moneta hasn't earned a penny in operating income since 1943, but somehow it doesn't seem to matter. In the last five years the price has fluctuated between 6 cents a share and 22 cents a share. Where else are you going to find asset values like this?

Let me tell you about another penny stock that will illustrate some points that I want to make. This was back in the early days. There was this jewel called Arctic Gold and Silver mines. When I bought it I remember thinking that the name was worth the 46 cents a share I was paying. I was wrong. The company was delisted and I wrote off the investment. But it wasn't a total loss. I had this rather attractive stock certificate that they had mailed me. In those days they still mailed you the stock certificate. I was going to frame it on the wall. It would make a wonderful conversation piece, but it wasn't to be. I never got around to framing it because about a year later Arctic Gold and Silver mines rose from the dead. In Canada, mining companies can reconstitute themselves. If they pay their back taxes and fees, they can reclaim their charter, mining claims, and listing. Provided no one has acquired their claims in the interim. This happens more often than you would think. Arctic Gold and Silver mines was back in action, but I was no longer a believer. When the stock had struggled back to about 25% of what I had paid for it, I took the money and ran. The stock was delisted again, this time forever. I now regret sending back the stock certificate, it would look wonderful on the wall. The amount I received for the stock was trivial. In those days my standard investment was 500 shares.

At this point you are probably wondering how it is possible for penny mining stocks to survive for years and indeed decades without any operating income. It is tied up with the ability of penny mining stocks and penny mining stocks alone of all other investment categories to hibernate or go into suspended animation. It isn't unusual for a penny mining stock to have only three employees, the president, the secretary, and the geologist who usually doubles as the vice president. Until recent years it was possible for a determined president to operate a bare bones operation like this for as little as $250,000 a year or less. Today it can be done for $500,000 a year or less. Only the fact that penny mining stocks are the purest asset plays on earth allows this type of set up to be feasible.

Since they typically earn no income, the normal means of funding by a broker-promoted secondary offering doesn't work for mining stocks once they have been around for a few years and their stock is still selling for pennies. The standard method by which penny mining stocks raise capital is by way of what is called a private placement. In this model the president solicits money directly from private investors every year. Under ideal circumstances it can work like this. The president invites say four to six serious investors out to investigate the mining site. If he is smart, he will provide each investor with one of those cute geologist's hammers and a jeweler's loupe with a chain so that they can wear their new status symbol around their necks. A jeweler's loupe is a small ten-power magnifying glass that is the status symbol of three professions; jewelers, coin collectors, and geologists. Each profession loves these status symbols and never misses an opportunity to employ them with great ostentation. At the mine site the investors will be invited to chip off rock samples with their cute little hammers and examine them under their jeweler's loupe. For lunch they go down to the lake and have a picnic. If they are lucky, they can watch soaring eagles capturing fish while they lunch. How do I know that there is a lake? There are hundreds of thousands of lakes in Canada; I kid you not. Every mine I have ever owned has been within sight of a lake and two of them were located on islands in the middle of a lake. In the afternoon, time will be set aside for some fishing, and late in the afternoon or evening there will be fried fish over an enormous fire. If the weather is good, getting the investors to write a check is like shooting fish in a barrel. A determined president can keep his company solvent for years using this technique.

Let's now take a look at the type of profits that penny mining stocks can generate by looking at three of my recent successes.

Exall Resources was a stock that was an old favorite of mine. I had sold it twice before at a profit. This time I purchased it at 18 cents a share. Exall was now under new management and the new management had decided that it would re-deploy its assets into the oil and gas sector and place all its gold assets into a new gold company that would be called Gold Eagle mines and then spin Gold Eagle mines off to Exall's owners. This was fine with me. I am a big energy fan. Now Gold Eagle's mine was located in the fabulous Red Lake mining camp. This is Canada's most prolific gold mining area. At this time a new drilling program was underway at Gold Eagle. The stock was rising nicely, but nothing out of the ordinary. When suddenly the stock jumped overnight from about 30 cents a share to $1.20 a share. For an old salt like myself it wasn't too difficult to figure out what had happened. The arrival of the Northern Miner provided the answer. The drill program was a success and reported high-grade gold intercepts, much higher than anybody had expected. The president hastily informed the owners that the program to spin off Gold Eagle had been canceled, a wise decision. At this point my normal procedure would be to take the money and run. Normally after a report like this the stock blows off and then declines. A decline back to the 60 cents to 80 cents a share range would be normal. But this was the Red Lake mining camp and the core samples were very rich. Against my better judgment I held on. To my considerable surprise the stock didn't decline as I expected; it continued to rise. There were now three drills on site instead of one. This was highly unusual action for a penny mining stock, which must hoard their limited resources. And they were reporting bonanza grades. It looked like Gold Eagle was a mine in the making. I was holding on. As this is being written, Exall Resources is selling for $2.00 a share. Not bad for an 18-cents-a-share investment and this move may not be over. Exall Resources 2005 annual report was a joy to read it began like this.

> Our company has not seen a year like 2005 in its entire 71-year history. With a major discovery at the Gold Eagle property, the very property that formed the foundation of Exall's incorporation as a company on February 13, 1934, we have come full circle co-incident with a very exciting time in the gold business.

But the part I liked best in the annual report was the part that said that Exall's stock had climbed 1,100% during the second half of 2005 based on positive drill results.

Another favorite that I am very keen on is Canadian Zinc. The saga of Canadian Zinc, and it truly is a saga, begins with the famous Hunt brothers and their attempt to corner the silver market in 1980. In the process the price of silver was driven to $50 an ounce. As this was going on the Hunt brothers were building what is today's Prairie Creek mine in Canada's Northwest Territories. The Hunt brothers sank $50,000,000 into building the mining infrastructure, which was 90% complete when the Hunt brothers declared bankruptcy and lost the mine. Over the years a total $100,000,000 has been spent to build the infrastructure that is now complete. The ore body is extraordinary, 11.8 million tonnes of lead, zinc, and silver. If silver were a base metal the deposit would probably rank as the richest base metal deposit in the North American Continent that wasn't in production. The deposit contains 70 million ounces of silver, three billion pounds of zinc and 2.2 billion pounds of lead.

I know what you are thinking: "Fred, how much did you have to pay to buy into this treasure trove?" I made my initial buy in 2002 for nine cents a share, but my average cost is now 20 cents a share. As this is being written, silver is selling for about $10 a ounce, zinc is selling for $1.02 a pound, and lead is selling for 53 cents a pound. Now if my figures are right you come up with a total ore body value of about $4.86 billion rounded. Currently Canadian Zinc has about 93.4 million shares issued. Therefore each share represents about $52 in ore value. As this is being written, Canadian Zinc is selling for about 80 cents a share. The best is yet to come. Now the astute reader is going to point out that what is really important isn't the value of the ore body, but whether it can be extracted at a profit. And this is of course true, but when you own 40-50 penny mining stocks and each position is considerably less than 1% of your investment capital, you need a quick and useful indicator of value, and this is one of the best. For years I struggled with this problem. There are many mining claims for which no reliable ore estimates exist. How do you estimate value? For a real estate appraiser this was a serious matter that I couldn't resolve.

One day, plus or minus two years from the time of my Koger Equity crisis, I was reading the Northern Miner. I was trying to make sense out of the core drilling samples that had just been reported to the press by a company that I was following, but of course I wasn't having any luck. The only thing I know about geology I learned in a college course. As I agonized over the data, the second great revelation of my stock market career occurred. In a flash I realized that penny mining companies weren't mining companies at all unless they were producers; and this is very rare. They are in reality real-estate companies in drag. They are "location plays." And I had always been too stupid to figure it out.

In real estate the classic location play is raw acreage. You find out in what direction the city is growing and you drive out in that direction until you reach the point where the land is sold by the acre rather than by the lot, then you just buy and wait for the city's growth to reach you. Penny mining stocks only asset is their mining claim, which is real estate. And the value of that mining claim is overwhelmingly determined by its location in a mining camp or proven mineral trend. When a mining camp reports a rich strike, all the mining stocks go up in value and the cheapest stocks go up the most. Armed with this knowledge I was able to take bigger positions and bet with more confidence than had ever been possible before.

There is one last penny market play that I have to tell you about. The reason why is that it is the greatest profit maker I have ever had on a percentage basis. It started out in an unusual manner.

In the year 2001 I bought a little jewel called Pioneer Metals for 12 cents a share. I liked the stock because it had a nice package of properties and it was being run by the highly regarded mining promoter Stephen Sorensen. A year later in 2002 the owners of Pioneer Metals received a most intriguing letter. We were informed that the company had decided to spin off its uranium properties into a new corporation to be called UEX. I was only vaguely aware that it even had uranium properties. I had purchased the stock because it had an interesting stable of gold properties. But what blew me away was their brilliant analysis of the coming boom in uranium. Until that time uranium didn't even appear on my radarscope. By the time I finished reading the report, I was a raging bull on uranium. At that time uranium was selling for about $18 a pound, today it is selling for $45.50 a pound. The shortage is so acute that $60 a pound is in the bag in the next two years; at its birth in 2002 UEX was blessed with about 247,000 very strategic acres in Canada's Athabasca basin in northern Saskatchewan. The Athabasca basin is the richest, but not the largest, uranium camp in the world and produces about 30% of the world's uranium. I was so impressed with UEX's potential that after the spin off, I increased my position by an additional 25%. Because the value of Pioneer Mines was worth more after the spin off than when I purchased it, I decided that for accounting purposes I would regard the cost of the spin off shares as zero. Currently Pioneer Metals is selling for about 57 cents a share. When I consolidated the free spin off shares with my purchased shares of UEX the average cost of my position was seven cents a share.

I wasn't the only one who was impressed with the potential of this new creation. From the moment it went public, its rise was relentless. UEX currently sells for $4.25 a share. My investment has increased in value about 60 times and the sky is still the limit. As I have stated before, it is possible for an investment to be too good to be true if people are unaware of its existence. The penny mining stock universe is the secret citadel of stocks that the investing public would regard as being too good to be true if they knew it existed. Where else can you routinely make microbets or chump change investments and get returns like this? I rest my case.

WHAT A BARGAIN LOOKS LIKE

PE RATIO (PRICE TO EARNINGS) BELOW 15
P/CF (PRICE TO CASH FLOW) BELOW 8
P/S (PRICE TO SALES RATIO) BELOW 1.5
P/B (PRICE TO BOOK VALUE) BELOW 1.5
DCR (DEBT COVERAGE RATIO) AT LEAST 1.2
DEBT TO CAPITALIZATION RATIO BELOW 33%
ANNUAL 5 YEAR HIGH & LOW IN THE LOW RANGE

Almost never will all the above indicators be in bargain territory. What is important is that the weight of the indicators be in bargain territory. For many years I was little more than a low PE investor, and that is where I hung my hat. As the nineties began there was so much fraud with earnings that I could no longer rely on them. I then placed primary reliance on P/S and P/B indicators because they were tamper proof. The annual five-year highs and lows for any stock are hugely important. You can almost earn a living in the stock market by doing nothing more than buying stocks when they approach their five-year lows and selling them when they approach their five-year highs. What isn't important and what will kill you is the ever-popular profit margin and operating margin indicators. Investors have always placed great importance in these margins. The problem with these indicators is that they will always lead you to overpriced blue chips and highfliers. Is it not logical that highfliers will have fabulous operating and profit margins?

What will have the worse margins you ever saw are the gutter stocks that will make you serious money. Stocks that have been crushed and pulverized so badly that you will need a ladder to take you to the bottom of the crater where they reside.

THE LEAP OPTION STRATEGY

Options are a highly dangerous investment tool. For years on balance I was a loser with options. What would happen again and again is that I would hit a home run with options just often enough to keep myself in the game. Options gave me what is of paramount importance to all speculators: leverage. If your goal is to make big bucks, then you must be able to buy or control huge blocks of stocks at chump change prices. I wanted the enormous leverage and the ability to go short or hedge a bet that only options provide. This book isn't about options and most people would be better off if they never touched options. The true riverboat gambler, however, can't ignore the awesome leverage that this tool gives you. Under no circumstances should anyone engage in option trading who hasn't read at least one book on options. Unless you are familiar with options, much of what I have to say in this section won't make much sense to you. Not to worry, feel free to ignore the whole section on options.

Options are broken down into two broad categories called Call options, which are the right to purchase a stock at an agreed upon strike price at a stated future date, and Puts, which are options that confer the right to sell a stock at a an agreed upon strike price at a stated future date, all options are written for 100 shares. If you were bullish on a stock, you would buy a Call, and if you are bearish about a stock and think that the price will fall, you would buy a Put. In other words you can make money with options whether the stock goes up or down.

Options are written for periods of 30, 60, 90, and 180-day periods. There are now long-term options written for as long as 30 months that expire every January of the appropriate year and they are called leaps. The only options that I recommend buying are these long-term leap options. The book that turned it around for me was *Using Options To Buy Stocks*, by Dennis Eisen. This book is absolute must reading for all option players. Options are valued by using a complicated mathematical formula called the Black-Scholes formula, which was named after its creators. The Black-Scholes model was invented before leap options were created in 1990, and as a result, the model ignores the possible long-term changes or growth rates in the underlying stock that might occur during the option's existence. With the classic short-term options this doesn't matter because there isn't enough time for the underlying stock to deviate substantially in value. This matter is considerably aggravated by the fact that the overwhelming mass of option trading is concentrated in the option class that is the closest to its expiration date. The reason for this is that the vast mass of option traders are playing cute little option games in which the value of the underlying stock is almost totally ignored and of little concern. What is of absolute concern is paying the lowest possible option price or premium, even if the option is going to expire in a matter of days.

The world of options is a highly complex world in which there are more intricate strategies than you can shake a stick at. These strategies have exotic names, they are called straps and straddles and spreads and butterflies. Mathematical types are suckers for these complex strategies and are all to often led to their doom by the alluring complexities of these strategies. It enables them to do what they have always wanted to do: which is to ignore the fact that there is an underlying stock involved. These people don't want to analyze the stock; they want to play cute little option games. For these people the stock is a nuisance.

Eisen's book showed me the truth, the light, and the way to consistent profits with options. The strategy is simplicity itself. Above all else, options are about leverage and you are a home run hitter. You ignore all the cute option games and buy the leap option with the longest remaining time without regard to how high the premium is. In short-term options the premium is everything. In long-term options time is everything. You need time for the market to realize that it has mispriced your stock and time for the big move to develop. The longer the time period, the greater the certainty that the Black-Scholes model has mispriced the value of the option.

Let's now consider two additional option strategies. The first is the wildly popular "covered call writing". In this strategy you write what are called "at the money calls" on a stock that you already own. The myth is that this simplistic strategy will earn you 20% a year. The assumption is that on an annual basis the premium on "at the money calls" will be around 20 % a year, and there are times when this will actually occur, but these times are rare indeed. Remember that we have to factor in the many times that our underlying stock will decline by more than the premium that you are receiving. In the real world, what you will discover is that you will probably net about 10% a year on a consistent basis with this strategy, which as you will recall is the long-term expectation for the stock market as a whole.

I forgot to tell you the rest of the myth. Not only are you, genius that you are, getting 20% a year on this incredibly simplistic strategy, but the jerks who are on the other side of the transaction are losing money on 90% of their call options. Pretty cute, huh?

I have more problems with this than you would believe. "Covered call writing" is the most popular option strategy that exists and not by a country mile, but by ten country miles. How rational is it to believe that there is this apparently inexhaustible army of jerks on the other side of the transaction who are losing money 90% of the time and who never wise up? Just who are these drooling imbeciles? They are home run hitters like me and hedgers. If you are a good home run hitter you can lose money 70% - 80% of the time and still be successful in options. Or if you are a hedger, it doesn't matter to you if the option expires worthless because you bought it for insurance or as part of a complex option strategy.

For my money there is only one scenario where covered call writing really makes sense and that is when you own a stock that you really like, but which you feel is temporarily overpriced and you don't want to sell it. Covered call writing makes sense in this scenario.

Let's take a real life example; I own a shipping company called OMI Corporation that I am very keen on. I purchased this little jewel at $7.57, it is now selling at $19.28, and the pundits say that shipping stocks should now be sold because this highly cyclical boom and bust business is past its peak. My suspicion is that the pundits are right. My problem is that in a market that is selling at 19 times earnings, OMI is selling at 5.69 times earnings. In other words, it is a screaming bargain and I just love how the management has positioned the company. Their fleet is a mix of 48 tankers and product carriers, which is the term for the specialized tankers that carry refined petroleum. Every ship in the fleet is now double-hulled and the average ship in the fleet is less than three years old. In addition, the company has just completed its third consecutive year of record profits. Management has offset much of the risk by putting 30 of its ships on long-term time charter. I also love the fleet mix. The company has wisely refused to get into the VLCC (very large crude carrier) market. Most of its ships are the so-called Suezmax and Panamax ships; these are the terms for the largest ships that can transit the Suez and the Panama canals. There are important competitive advantages for ships that can transit these canals. Lastly they have wisely, in my opinion, built up their fleet of the product carriers that can carry refined oil. Oil tankers can only carry crude oil; they aren't equipped to carry refined products. In a world of growing refinery shortages, this may be a very shrewd move. How can you sell a stock like this even if you think it will go down?

My favorite option strategy is the notorious "naked put"

option. There are two absolute caveats about writing naked puts. First, the stock must be a bargain in your estimation at the price you have contracted to buy it, and you must be ready and able to buy the stock at that price. Naked puts are regarded as a highly dangerous option and so-called experts are always warning people against it.

Let's take a look at my latest naked put transaction. I recently wrote naked puts on XTO oil corp. the stock was selling at $42.14 a share. The put was a Jan. $50 put of 2008. My premium for each put contract of 100 shares was $10.20 or $1,020. As soon as I wrote the put, $1,020 for each put contract was deposited into my account. This transaction didn't cost me a single dime and if it works out, it will never cost me a single dime. The worse case scenario is that in Jan. 2008 XTO is selling for less than $50, if that occurs, I am obligated to purchase the stock at $50 a share or a total of $5,000, but the day I wrote the contract I received a premium of $10.20 a share or $1,020. Therefore my true cost to purchase a share of XTO is $39.80 if you will recall that on the date I wrote the naked put XTO was selling for $42.14 a share. The worse case scenario has me purchasing the stock at a discount of $2.34 a share. The best-case scenario is that in Jan. 2008 XTO is selling above $50 a share in which case the $1,020 is mine to keep and I don't have to purchase anything. How can you beat that? Unless you are familiar with options, this strategy won't make sense to you.

Now I know what you are thinking, you are thinking: how can such a wonderful strategy be held in such disrepute? I have already commented on this problem, but this gives me another chance to get on my soapbox. Wall Street today as never before is dominated by armies of investors who aren't sincere and who are playing stupid little number games. These people know almost nothing about the companies that they are buying, and they couldn't care less. They believe they own a lottery ticket and not an ownership certificate; the only thing they care about is the next quarter's number. As a consequence, when the number isn't what is expected, these people get blown out of investments that they should have held on to and would have held onto if they knew anything about the company that they had invested in.

I believe in every company that I invest in and I am familiar with what the company is all about. I carefully read every annual report and highlight all the interesting points. I keep all the annual reports and refer to them as the year progresses. This is a big help to me when a stock I own declines. I can refer to the report and see if it makes sense to increase my position, which I often do. I try to attend all the annual meetings that are held in my locality, and I encourage you to do the same. Because I am a small-cap investor, more than 12 investors showing up for an annual meeting is a rare event. The last meeting I attended, only six owners showed up. We were treated like visiting royalty and it was a blast. If you adopt this attitude, you will be amazed at how much better you will do as an investor.

Now where were we before I got distracted? Now I remember, we were discussing why naked puts are frowned upon. As I was saying, most naked put investors are playing option games. They neither know anything about nor care about the stock they are writing a put on. They would regard the notion that they might actually want to own the stock that they have written the option on as quaint and laughable. As a result, when the put turns against them and they are forced to purchase the stock, they are appalled and are convinced that some great injustice has been done to them.

WALL STREET'S PET HATREDS

As I alluded to earlier, Wall Street worships in a very small cathedral. In this cathedral there is room for only two gods. The gods of big-cap growth stocks and high-tech growth stocks, all other stocks are regarded as being suitable only for losers. There is also a Wall Street hell. The denizens of this hell are listed below.

GOLD & SILVER
REAL ESTATE
NATURAL RESOURCES

The venom and hatred that Wall Street vomits out whenever gold is mentioned as a possible investment is remarkable to see,

I am always taken aback by it. You will immediately be castigated as being one of those stupid and ignorant gold bugs. With a look of icy contempt at your idiocy, they will launch into their standard diatribe. You will be sternly informed that gold is a "barbarous relic" and pays no interest. Therefore if you have a brain in your poor stupid head you will forget this madness and invest in big-cap and high-tech stocks like everybody else who has his head screwed on straight.

The attack against silver is identical to that of gold, but is carried out with less venom. To put it simply, the silver market is too small to be of major concern.

The attitude toward real estate is more patronizing. It is simply dismissed as an inferior investment. If you stretched things it might be a suitable investment for widows and orphans, but except for them it isn't regarded as a serious investment. As a result of this attitude, it was possible for decades to earn a total return on REIT stocks that was amazingly high. All good things must come to an end. The end came when Standard & Poor's decided to include REITs in their index. Almost overnight I went from being able to buy high quality REITs that were yielding dividends in the 8% to 10% area to today's 6% plus. All in all I am sorry that they were ever discovered. In an amazingly short period of time REITs also went in a straight shot from being an inferior investment that shouldn't be bought to being an inferior investment that shouldn't be bought because it was now overpriced and therefore not a good investment in Wall Street's eyes.

I am of the opinion that the reason for Wall Street's negative attitude on gold, silver, and real estate is that there is an "institutional memory" on the Street that regards these investments as competition, and therefore threats that must be attacked at every opportunity.

The case against natural resources is one of contempt rather than hatred. Natural resources are cyclical in nature and are historically low-profit enterprises. On Wall Street the word "cyclical" has very nasty connotations. According to Wall Street lore growth stocks can't be cyclical and therefore cyclical stocks must be anti growth. There is one important exception to this rule and that is the mighty oil and gas industry. Simply put, it is too important to be ignored.

THE REVOLUTIONS TO COME

It is now time to consider the revolutions to come, the revolutions that will make us rich if we have the foresight and courage to take advantage of them. As this is being written, a golden age of natural resources is underway. And it will last longer and rise higher than most people will believe is possible. The long age of abundant natural resources is coming to an end, and the age of natural resource scarcity has begun. The mantra of this new age will be that "wealth in the ground" will make you rich.

We are in the early stages of one of the greatest trend reversals in history. About ten years ago I was reading an article in the editorial page of the Northern Miner that had been written by a college professor. He had conducted a study of the price levels of natural resources going back to the start of the industrial revolution. His conclusion was that the price of natural resources had been falling steadily after you subtract the effect of inflation since the 1820's when the industrial revolution had its first serious impact on the mining industry. As soon as I read his article, I knew he was correct. The concentrated impact of a host of new inventions, led by the steam engine, to drain the mines and grind the ore to powder and the coming of more advanced high explosives has led to almost two centuries of falling prices in real terms. The longer any trend is in effect, the more violent the reversal is when it occurs. If for no other reason than it is impossible for people to believe that a trend reversal is possible.

For reasons that will become clear, our study of natural resources will be broken into two segments. First, we will analyze the oil and gas industry, and then we will consider the metals separately.

Fred Carach

THE LAW THAT FAILED

There is nothing more hysterical than trying to tell an economist that the world is running out of oil. He will glare at you with an icy contempt that would stop a charging bull elephant dead in his tracks. You will be informed in no uncertain terms that because of the law of supply and demand, only temporary shortages are possible and that in the long run demand will create its own supply. If you should bring up the inconvenient fact that new oil discoveries have been falling since 1970, he will dismissively wave his hand at you while informing you that there are millions of places in the world that have not been looked at yet and today's higher prices will result in a future avalanche of new discoveries.

As this is being written this is still the prevailing orthodox view, but this view is slowly starting to crumble. The truth of the matter is that the world has been witnessing the failure of the law of supply and demand for more than 30 years; and amazingly few people are aware of this fact. The law of supply and demand is one of the most powerful of all economic laws and is regarded by almost everyone as an invincible law, but this law is more vulnerable than people believe, and it rests on only two pillars. The first pillar is that rising prices will result in what economists call "demand destruction" as buyers either stop buying the product or shift to substitutes. The second pillar is that rising prices will result in an avalanche of increasing production. When today's oil industry is analyzed, one is confronted with the massive failure of the law of supply and demand stretching back more than 30 years.

It is hard to believe, but in 1970 oil was selling for about $2.00 a barrel and world consumption of oil was about 45 million barrels of oil per day. As this is being written, oil is selling for about $60 a barrel and world consumption is about 85 million barrels a day. A staggering price increase of 30 times has resulted in no demand destruction whatsoever. Indeed consumption has almost doubled.

Both pillars in the law of supply and demand now lie in a heap of ruins at our feet. Only one inescapable conclusion can be drawn from this, and that is that the law of supply and demand has stopped working for oil, and the question is: why? The correct answer is that the law of supply and demand has always had two caveats which economists have a very strange habit of ignoring. The first caveat is that substitutes are available. As we are all well aware, there are no readily available substitutes for oil. And the second caveat is that the potential supply isn't fixed or finite, but for all practical real world purposes infinite. And what is very, very troubling is that it is becoming more and more apparent that the supply of oil is fixed and finite, and that we are scraping the bottom of the barrel.

When last seen our crazed economist was pointing dramatically at imaginary hills that only he could see and hysterically screaming that the law of supply and demand always works, and that there was "gold in them thar hills". I think he meant oil. I was going to try to reason with him, but I would have had to tell him that I majored in economics in college and there was a real possibility that if I told him that, I wouldn't leave his presence alive. It is a remarkable fact that those who know the least about oil are the most convinced that peak oil is a fraud, and the economists are the very worst.

I know what you are thinking. You are thinking that maybe the crazed economist is right, what about all the millions of places we haven't explored yet? The brutal truth is that we have looked almost everywhere and come up dry. When you tell people this, they flatly refuse to believe you.

THE FINAL DAYS OF ANCIENT SUNLIGHT

Oil and gas as well is nothing more than ancient sunlight that has been entombed in the fossilized bodies of ancient plants and plant algae and mutated into oil and gas over a period of eons. In the case of oil there were two great generating periods in which all of the world's oil deposits were formed. The first period occurred about 150 million years ago, and the second period occurred about 90 million years ago. In both these periods vast blooms of microscopic plants formed in certain favorable ancient seas. As they died, entombed within them was the energy they had captured from the sun. They created a submarine rain of organic matter onto the sea floors so thick that they formed in layers, which under ideal conditions blocked out oxygen. If the layers were heavy enough, they would sink to the depth of what is called the oil window. For oil to form, these fossilized plants must be trapped in an oxygen deprived sedimentary rock at a depth of between 7,500 feet and 15,000 feet below the surface, the so called oil window for vast periods of geologic time where they are transformed by heat and pressure into petroleum. When these conditions are present, the result is called "source rock". Above 7,500 feet, there isn't enough heat and pressure to form petroleum, and below 15,000, the heat and pressure is too great and the oil is destroyed and converted into natural gas.

Now oil can only be born at this depth, but it doesn't have to remain at this depth. It is common for oil to seep to the surface. It is also common for the forces of erosion and uplift to result in oil fields being found at or near the surface. Unfortunately for us there are additional severe requirements that must be met for petroleum to be extracted. Embedded within the source rock must be a rock that is called "reservoir rock". This is a porous rock in which oil can collect and when drilled will release its oil to the surface. The third requirement is a "cap rock", which stops the oil from escaping from the reservoir rock. Fourth, there must be a "trap", a structure in the rocks - usually a giant fold - into which the oil flows to be trapped under the cap rock. And fifth, the structure must be leak proof; fractures in the rock, which are called faults, will result in the oil seeping out and being lost forever. The ultimate prize for oil geologists which they spend their lives looking for are the big dome-shaped entrapments called "anticlines" which meet all the above requirements except for the all important fifth one, that the anticlines be leak proof. Here and here alone can oil be discovered.

These are the brutal and exacting requirements that must be met for oil to be present. Only a terrifyingly small percentage of the earth's surface can meet the above requirements. Consider the most basic requirement sediments with a depth of at least 7,500 feet before you hit bedrock. Most of the world flunks this test big time. Consider the fact that most of the world's mountains are less than 7,500 feet in height. An example of a typical area that has almost no sediment that comes to mind is New York City. If you swing a pick, you will hit bedrock. That is why it is such a wonderful place to build skyscrapers.

The vast deep-water ocean basins, which occupy 60% of the earth's surface, are losers that can be written off. The reason why they can be written off is that nowhere in these deep-water basins does the sediments exceed a depth of 3,000 feet and thus they fail the all important sedimentary depth requirement. However, there is an additional 11% of the earth's ocean surface which covers the shallow water continental shelves of the earth and does meet the sedimentary requirements, and these are some of our richest oil deposits. The Gulf of Mexico, the North Sea and the Persian Gulf are outstanding examples of this.

People have no concept of how diligent and how thorough the oil geologists have been in their relentless quest for new oil discoveries and how little has escaped them. By the 1920's they knew that oil existed on Alaska's north slope. And by the 1950's they had invented and were installing the world's first marine drilling platforms in the Gulf of Mexico. Just ask yourself why any oil company would risk drilling in the hurricane plagued Gulf of Mexico in the 1950's. There is only one answer. They were already scraping the bottom of the barrel. By 1945 the first aerial geological maps had became available and by 1950 all the anticlines that were visible from the surface in the United States had been mapped and drilled. And by the 1960's the entire land surface of the earth had been mapped by satellites and every visible surface anticline located.

PEAK OIL

M. King Hubbert was the visionary who invented the concept of peak oil. In 1956 this geophysicist made the then astounding prediction that the United States would reach its peak oil production sometime between 1966 and 1972 and then go into irreversible decline. At that time drillers were hitting gushers everywhere they looked and the concept of peak oil seemed absurd. Critics lined up three times around the block to attack him. The actual peak of U.S. oil production occurred in 1970 and has been declining ever since.

The complex mathematical equations that he used to predict this filled pages, but the gist of his analysis is that the production peak for any oil reservoir will occur when almost exactly half of the economically extractable oil has been extracted from the reservoir. Since that time, country after country has passed peak production and gone into decline more or less as the Hubbert formula predicted.

Today his disciples are carrying on his work. His leading disciple is the geophysicist Kenneth S. Deffeyes, who in 2001 wrote the book *Hubbert's Peak: The Impending World Oil Shortage*. This book is absolute must reading for anyone who is investing in oil. Deffeyes has predicted on his website that peak oil production occurred in December 2005, because of the way oil production works, new production is constantly coming on stream and old production is constantly declining, it will be several years before we know if this prediction is correct.

The peak oil boys have powerful evidence on their side. They have the facts. Let's take a look at some of these facts. Today the world consumes about 85 million barrels a day. This is a terrifying figure when you consider that every day we are consuming an ocean of oil. For this consumption to be sustained, we need to discover the super giant fields that can alone sustain us on a constant basis, but we aren't finding them. A giant oil field is defined as a field of at least one billion barrels; a super giant has at least ten billion barrels. The largest oil field ever discovered was the fabulous Ghawar field in Saudi Arabia with proven reserves of 87 billion barrels.

Among the last great proven super giants ever discovered were Alaska's Prudoe Bay and the North Sea fields, which were both discovered by 1970. Prudoe Bay is now in decline and the North Sea fields are now reporting declining production. Since 1970 only two new super giants have been discovered. The smallest is Kazakhstan's Caspian Sea Kashagan field that was discovered in 1999 and has an estimated size of 10-13 billion barrels.The other was Mexico's Cantarell oil field. Which was discovered in 1976 in the Gulf of Mexico off the Yucatan coast with an estimated reserve of 17 to 20 billion barrels. In 2006 the Mexican government announced that Cantarell, one of the youngest proven super giants ever discovered, was already in decline.

Deffeyes says that it appears that there is only one possible super giant left to be discovered, and it is located in the South China Sea. It has never been explored because the surrounding countries can't agree on who owns it. If there is anything worth fighting for, this is it. We used to be able to discover super giants every time we turned around, but now we can't discover them anywhere.

Most of the world's oil was discovered in a magical 40-year block of time between 1930 and 1970. Since 1970, every decade has seen less oil discovered than the preceding decade. This is in spite of the fact that we now have the most advanced oil technology we have ever possessed. How is it possible that we were finding more oil using the primitive technology of the 1930's and 1940's than we can find today? The last year that we discovered more oil than we consumed was 1986. In a typical year we now consume about three or four barrels of oil for every barrel of oil that we discover. For example, in the year 2005, we discovered 10 billion barrels of oil and consumed 30 billion barrels. Today an appalling 80% of global oil production comes from fields discovered prior to 1970, and world consumption increases every year like clockwork by about 2%.

It gets worse; another very disturbing fact that the oil in abundance crowd ignores in their monumental ignorance is that about 80% to 90%, depending upon your source, of the world's oil reserves aren't owned by the big multinational oil corporations, which is what everyone assumes, but by the so-called NOCs. These are the state-owned national oil companies of the world, most of which aren't our buddies, and they have no interest whatsoever in providing us with cheap oil. Their only interest is in providing us with the most expensive oil possible. In many cases they have neither the technology nor the capital to increase production, and indeed have declining production. Venezuela is the classic example of this; it supplies the United States with 12% of our oil imports and its oil production is in decline. To an ever-increasing degree, Exxon Mobile and the rest of the multi-national oil companies are becoming the flunkies of the NOCs and aren't allowed to own or develop the oil fields. Their only role is to transport, refine and market the oil of the NOCs. Just think through the implications of that.

THE SAUDI MYTH

Every time the subject of peak oil is discussed, the Saudi myth is brought up. "Not to worry," we are told, "we can rely on the inexhaustible oil reserves of Saudi Arabia, why you can just push a stick in the ground and the oil will gush up." The second book that is must reading for oil investors is Matthew R. Simmon's 2005 book, *Twilight In The Desert*. In this tour de force Simmons pulverizes this belief of inexhaustible Saudi oil with a sledgehammer.

The Saudi oil miracle is based on five old Saudi super giants led by the mighty Ghawar field that have produced 90% of all Saudi oil production. Three additional giant fields make up almost all the remaining oil production. These eight fields are the ball game and they are all terrifyingly old for oil fields. They are all 40 to 60 years old. The assumption has always been that there were more oil giants in Saudi Arabia just waiting to be discovered when the Saudis finally made the effort. The shocking truth is that the Saudis have made the effort and come up dry. Starting in the late 1960's a major comprehensive effort was made to explore the entire Saudi land mass. The last major field that was discovered in Saudi Arabia was the Shaybah field in 1967, since then they have discovered nothing of consequence, certainly nothing to replace their eight aging giants. As Simmons puts it:

> The real history of Saudi Arabian oil exploration has been rather different than conventional wisdom has assumed. The lack of additional great finds since the late 1960's was not due to a lack of effort. The effort was there. The oil was not. Pg. 37

Then there is the phony baloney reporting of reserves. According to Simmons, for the last 17 years the Saudis reported reserves have been pegged at about 260 billion barrels. However, during these same years more than 46 billion barrels of oil have been produced from this base.

There is also the famous OPEC oil miracle of 1982. In that year OPEC decided to allocate each member's cartel quota based on their reported reserves. In the next couple of years a succession of OPEC oil ministers announced, while giggling stupidly at the press, massive increases in their countries oil reserves from already discovered oil fields and not from new discoveries. They were giggling stupidly because they couldn't believe that anyone would be stupid enough to believe their numbers. They were wrong! People would be stupid enough to believe their numbers. By the time the ministers had stopped giggling stupidly at each other, OPEC reserves had magically increased by a staggering 300 billion barrels, today the "not to worry crowd" point to these numbers as if they were pure gold. What a bunch of jerks!

Perhaps the greatest blindness is the "addition without subtraction" technique that is being utilized to prove that there is no oil problem. People simply add the new production that is presumed to be coming on stream to current production and conclude that there is no problem. What these clowns fail to realize is that in the natural resource realm resource depletion is a never-ending force that must be reckoned with. There are of course great divergences in the depletion rate from field to field but most of the world's oil fields are depleting at a rate of between 4% and 8% a year. The oil industry needs to run very fast just to stand still.

Consider this, in the 1940's the United States was the world's greatest oil producer and exporter. One of the most important reasons why Japan attacked the United States in 1941 was that we had declared an oil embargo on Japan. And our oil embargo was threatening to strangle them. As late as 1960, the United States was almost self-sufficient in oil production. Today we are forced to import a disturbing 60% of our oil.

When the mighty Prudoe Bay oil field came into production in the 1970's it supplied 25% of the nation's oil needs. Today it supplies only 8% of the nation's oil and its production is dropping off of a cliff. At its peak it was producing 1.5 million barrels a day. Today its production has fallen 73% to 400,000 barrels a day. This is the horrific impact of depletion. We ignore it at our peril.

Now I know what you are thinking! You are thinking: "Gee, Fred, all this sounds very impressive, but haven't you overlooked something? What about the humongous U.S. oil inventory that we are holding in our storage tanks?" What about that? What about those mysterious inventories that are somehow always above their five-year average and are always bulging at the seams and threatening to burst at any moment and flood the nation with oil? And which of course are always being reported upon with great seriousness as proof that there is nothing to worry about.

It is nothing more of course than the stupid twaddle of the uninformed. Raymond James & Assoc. is a wonderful source of useful data on the petroleum industry. You can find their excellent reports on the Internet. In their latest report they stipulate that the current U.S. oil storage supply is about 34 days. And for the last five years this figure has never exceeded about 45 days.

"Gee, Fred, if that is the case, why are they making such a big deal about this number?" There are two reasons. First, these people are as dumb as a fence post; unless the fence post is having a bad day. Second, this number is one of the very few numbers that "the oil in abundance crowd" can point to.

In the old days when the United States was self-sufficient in oil, this number had some relevance. Somebody needs to tell these so-called experts that we are no longer self-sufficient in oil. There is of course another reason that Matthew Simmons and the rest of the peak oil boys keep bringing up and that is the amazing lack of hard, useful data. In the petroleum universe data is treated like a military secret.

The last book that is absolute must reading for oil investors is Richard Heinberg's 2003 book, *The Party's Over*. This is the most terrifying book I have ever read. The front cover shows a man pointing an oil pump at his forehead as if it was a gun and he is ready to blow his brains out. Heinberg predicts not an oil crisis, but an oil holocaust. In the section of his book entitled a banquet of consequences, he points out that there are six billion people on this earth and that if the looming oil crisis is as bad as he predicts, four billion of these people will have to vanish.

In 1900 there were about two billion people on this earth and about 80% to 90% of this population engaged in farming. Not out of choice, but out of necessity. It took this much manual labor to grow enough food to feed the world's population.

Manual labor, however, wasn't enough, working with the farmers were the all important draft animals, a term that has almost been forgotten. Draft animals such as horses, mules, donkeys and oxen provided the heavy-duty horsepower so necessary for farming operations, and their manure was critical for fertilizer. It is interesting to note that the average sustained human power output is roughly one-twentieth of a horsepower. An additional interesting point is that in the year 1900 the growing of horse feed required one quarter of the total available cropland, or about 90 million acres. This cropland today has been largely converted into growing food for the growing human population or converted into subdivisions.

Then after 1900 the oil revolution hit and mechanized farming replaced draft animals. It is easy to believe that farm mechanization explains the agricultural revolution and the soaring production increases that occurred after 1900. It doesn't; it is only a partial explanation. Far more important was the petrochemical revolution. The petrochemical industry uses oil and natural gas as feedstocks to produce a vast array of commodities and products that only a few people realize are petrochemical based. Among these uses are plastics, herbicides, pesticides, and chemical fertilizer. The real basis of the farm revolution after 1900 was the massive use of pesticides and herbicides on agricultural land to kill off competing pest plants and crop devouring insects. Chemical fertilizers were also employed on a massive scale to increase productivity.

The use of these petrochemical products has resulted in huge increases in farm yields per acre in the 20th Century. These spiraling increases in farm productivity is what made possible the four billion extra people that the world has acquired since 1900.

If the oil crisis is as bad as Heinberg predicts, then farm productivity will go into a death spiral and at least four billion human beings will have to vanish. And it could be much worse, we not only no longer have the draft animals, but we also no longer have the cropland to feed them. Heinberg is quite coy about how this energy holocaust will be resolved, but the obvious answer is by nuclear war. If the Heinberg scenario occurs, the world is going to discover just how ruthless a soccer mom can be who has just discovered that she has to ride a bicycle to work because there is no gas to be had.

Case closed, and in my opinion case proven. In more than 40 years as a speculator I have never seen a surer thing than betting on an energy crisis. If there was ever a time to bet the ranch, this is that time.

TREND REVERSAL

Unlike the case for oil where the law of supply and demand has broken down completely, the law of supply and demand will always work for the metals complex because the supply of metals is for all practical purposes inexhaustible. The case for the metals isn't as powerful as is the case for oil & gas, but it is still a very powerful case. I have already sketched out some of the reasons for this position.

As is the case for oil, geologists and prospectors have been very diligent in the search for metals. The old timers missed very little in the way of easily accessible surface deposits. Most of the cheap low hanging fruit has been picked. It isn't generally realized, but most of the so-called new mineral discoveries of the last 20 years aren't as is generally assumed so-called new green-field discoveries, but are reexaminations of prospects that have been known for decades, if not generations. What happens is that sustained low prices and the exhaustion of cheap readily available ore results in the closing of these mines. When the next turn of the wheel occurs and metal prices skyrocket, miners return and re-explore the old discoveries. Many of the so-called new discoveries in Alaska and the Yukon for instance are within visual sighting of mining head frames that were built during the famous Yukon gold rush of the 19th century. In addition, the miners have a powerful new ally, the politically correct Greens. Since the environmentalist movement began, the Greens have been busily constructing a series of virtual Chinese walls around vast wilderness areas, which are designed to discourage and prevent new mining developments, and they have succeeded only too well.

As this is being written the entire metals complex is in a raging bull market and the Wall Street boys are standing around scratching their heads as they try to figure out why the metals haven't done their usual swan dive as they have been doing for almost two hundred years. The way it always used to work is that whenever metal prices boomed and profits were lush, the boom had a life expectancy of about 18 to 24 months before an avalanche of new production buried the miners, and it wasn't unusual for it to take 10 to 20 years before the economy could absorb all this new production. This guaranteed that the time of lush profits would be short and sweet and that the time of miserable profits would be interminable. And then the whole stupid cycle would repeat itself again and again.

A historic trend reversal is now underway. The greens have guaranteed that never again will an avalanche of new production bury the miners 18 to 24 months after the metals soar. The virtual Chinese wall of rules and regulations that they have erected has guaranteed that this can no longer occur. It now takes on average four to eight years for new green-field production to come on line, not 18 to 24 months. Those mining concerns that have production in being or where production can be brought into being because of Green acquiescence will be fabulous profit generators.

There is a further important distinction to be made about the mining industry. The 20th century witnessed the birth of a new type of mining that the world had never witnessed before, the open-pit mine. It has always been a stretch to call these operations mines. In reality they were vast earth moving operations that were pretending to be mines. The only thing that made these operations feasible was cheap energy. I am in agreement with Richard Heinberg that these open-pit operations may be 20th century dinosaurs. If this occurs, then a vast amount of metal production that the world takes for granted will be swept off the table and the classic hard rock mines will become fabulous cash cows. Now it goes without saying that metal prices will continue to fluctuate with the economy. The point to be made is that mines will earn greater profits for longer periods than has been the historical norm.

Another tremendous bullish factor for the mining industry is the rise of the so-called rapidly industrializing BRIC countries, Brazil, Russia, India, and China. Never before have more than

2.5 billion people entered the ranks of the advanced world. The demand of these people on the energy complex and the metals complex will be staggering. Consider the case of copper; the typical house has four hundred pounds of copper in it. About 151 pounds is plumbing related and the rest is electrical. It is no surprise to me that as this is being written the price of copper has risen to a new all-time high.

I am bullish on the entire base metals complex with one exception. That exception is aluminum. The problem is that refining aluminum is a horrific energy consumer and the very high-energy consumption may render aluminum uneconomic.

Coal and uranium are going to have fantastic futures. Oil and natural gas in the future will be too precious to be used to produce electricity, and coal and uranium are the only possible substitutes. How to convert coal into oil and natural gas has been known since Germany invented the process prior to the Second World War.

THE ANATOMY OF A RIVERBOAT GAMBLE

As these words are being written, I have just had a brainstorm. I am getting ready to make one of my famous riverboat gambles. It has occurred to me that I should digress from the subject at hand and take you through the process as it is occurring. I am going to show you the anatomy of a riverboat gamble as it is happening. It began today when I received my weekly copy of the Northern Miner. I am such a sicko that receiving the Northern Miner is one of the high points of my week. Is that sick or what?

I am a firm believer in dressing for the role. I am now wearing my wonderful southern plantation hat. Clenched between my teeth is one of those cute little cigarillos that Clint Eastwood smoked in his famous spaghetti westerns. I am also wearing a classy western bola tie with a polished agate stone, which is the size of my fist that I purchased at the world-famous annual Tucson Gem and Mineral Show. Did I ever tell you that I am a gem collector? And last but not least, I am wearing the most impossibly gaudy huge western belt buckle that you have ever seen. This belt buckle would make any rhinestone cowboy turn green with envy. As I look in the mirror I just can't believe how handsome I am. If my friends at the Mississippi Belle could see me now, I would knock them dead. But this isn't about how impossibly handsome I am. This is about me teaching you how to become a riverboat gambler like me, if you could ever be so lucky. I practice some of my favorite Clint Eastwood scowls in front of the mirror. After a heroic struggle, I finally manage to tear myself away from the mirror. I am now seated in front of my computer, the scene of some of my most famous riverboat triumphs. After giving the computer my best Clint Eastwood sneer, we are now ready to consider the riverboat gamble at hand.

The news in the Northern Miner that concerned me was a report on one of my old favorites, which I currently own for the third time, a little jewel called Campbell Resources.

Campbell Resources is up to its old tricks again and is in deep trouble. This is a stock that is constantly in trouble, which is why I like it. The astute reader will recall that some of my favorite plays are stocks that are bankruptcy candidates, or even better are emerging from bankruptcy. Campbell Resources is a copper-gold producer in the province of Quebec. Before I go any further it has occurred to me that I should tell you something about ore bodies.

There are certain metals that make a habit of appearing together in the same ore bodies. Lead, zinc, and silver are commonly found together in the same ore body and many copper mines contain a substantial amount of gold in their ore.

Campbell Resources was incorporated in 1950 and has about 107 million shares outstanding. It has an interesting portfolio of ten properties and its two major mines, the Joe Mann mine, and the Copper Rand mine are examples of copper-gold mines. It has struggled for years to make its operations at these two properties profitable with little success. The company is currently under the protection of the companies creditor arrangement act until May 31, a critical drilling program is currently underway. The company needs to find more ore. The success of this drilling program may determine whether the company lives or dies. I purchased the stock at 35 cents a share. The stock is now selling at 14 cents a share. Just take a gander at this stock's annual highs and lows.

```
2000  .35 - 4.50
2001  .26 - 1.05
2002  .29 -  .91
2003  .33 - 1.11
2004  .37 - 1.11
2005  .12 -  .35
```

How could you not love a stock like this? However, it could all go up in a puff of smoke on May 31. The question that I face, fellow riverboat gamblers, is should I double down my investment in Campbell Resources? As the ice water flows through my veins I coolly calculate the odds, and then with nerves of steel I double down my bet. There you have it, fellow riverboat gamblers, the professional in action! Welcome to my world.

Now I know what you are thinking! You know that there is a major flaw in my logic. The flaw is this, on May 31 Campbell Resources may go bankrupt and wipe out my entire investment. What kind of deal is that? You ask. You need to see what the riverboat gambler sees. The riverboat gambler knows that once you leave the world of math and science behind you, life is about probabilities and not certainties. No matter how much we deny it life is about probabilities, and we crave certainties. Life resembles a series of dice throws and these dice are made out of iron. No other substance will do. Life is like iron, cold, hard, and unforgiving. The dice could never have been made out of something pleasant and beautiful like gold. Why if you put a gold coin in your mouth and bite it, you will dent the coin. If you put an iron coin in your mouth and bite it, you will break your teeth. Therefore the dice of life and destiny are made out of iron.

We all refuse to believe how uncertain life is and therefore we are constantly left holding an empty bag when our certainties fail us. There are no rewards for betting that tomorrow will be like today, but there are huge rewards for those of us who are willing to bet that tomorrow won't be like today. There are two types of people in this world. Those who will pick up the iron dice of destiny and throw them, and those who will not. Those who won't are mere bystanders in life. Those who will pick up the iron dice of destiny and throw them have a chance, but not a certainty, of controlling their own destiny.

Above all else, the riverboat gambler knows what others are blind to; the dice are loaded in favor of the shooter. Inscribed on the iron dice of destiny in microscopic print is the following statement: Carefully research your investments and then buy everything that you like, the dice are loaded in your favor. This of course doesn't hold true for any single investment or roll of the dice, but it does hold true if you roll the dice again and again.

Consider the case of Campbell Resources; are the dice not loaded in my favor? If I was a chimp throwing darts, I would have a better than a 50-50 chance of winning. If you research your investments, the odds go up to at least 60%. My maximum downside is 100%. My maximum upside is unlimited of course, but a good bet is at least 300% to 1,000%. My risk capital in this play is about a quarter of 1% of my total investment capital. If I lose, I simply write off my losses on my tax return. You tell me, fellow riverboat gamblers, are the dice not loaded in my favor? Welcome to my world. Come on in. It is time to pick up the iron dice of destiny and start throwing them. Stop being a bystander, and most important of all, be sure to buy yourself one of those wonderful southern plantation hats. It helps to dress for the role.

THE WRATH OF ADAM SMITH

The last revolution to come that can earn us huge profits is what I choose to call "the wrath of Adam Smith", but it could just as easily be called the coming triumph of the gold bugs. Adam Smith is justly regarded as the father of economics, in 1776 he wrote his masterpiece, *The Wealth Of Nations*. The primary purpose of his book was to level an attack against the then prevailing economic doctrine of Mercantilism. This doctrine held that the way to national prosperity and power was to have a favorable balance of trade. The theory stated that if your exports exceed your imports, this would result in a flow of gold and silver into your country, and that you will also export your unemployment to your trading partners. In another words, it could be described as waging economic warfare against your trading partners, a war in which you would first steal their gold and silver and later their jobs as well.

Adam Smith argued is his work that in the long run this doctrine couldn't be made to work, that it was counterproductive and would lead to chronic warfare. In its place he advocated the concept of free trade. If you talk to most economists, they will tell you that Adam Smith's doctrine of free trade has swept the world. I don't know what cave they have been living in for the last 35 years or so, but I can assure you that Adam Smith would never buy it.

It all started to go terribly wrong in 1971 when the gold exchange standard that had been established at the Bretton Woods conference of 1944 was abolished and was replaced with the fiat money standard. Fiat money is paper money that isn't backed up by gold or silver.

If Adam Smith were alive today, he would look at the world and weep. What he would see isn't the free trade that he championed, but rampant Mercantilism.

The easiest way to prove this is simply to look at the United State's balance of trade. For more than 40 years now we have run an unfavorable balance of trade. If free trade was being practiced, such a thing would be impossible, but such a thing is very possible under Mercantilism. Under a regime of free trade, if the most advanced nation on earth trades with the most backward nation on earth over any extended time period, the trade between the two nations would balance out. Trade wouldn't be a zero sum game as it is under Mercantilism, but a win-win scenario as each nation would specialize in producing whatever it had a comparative advantage in producing, and both nations would be wealthier and better off by trading with each other than they would be by not trading with each other.

Let's do a thought experiment. Let's imagine that this is the 19th century, the gold standard is in effect and Advanistan has just discovered Backwardistan. At first, things look very bad for Backwardistan. Their people are dazzled by the highly desirable industrial products of Advanistan and a river of gold flows out of their country to pay for these highly desirable products, but as the gold flows out of their country the money supply is in effect shrinking, which means that there is less money to purchase these highly desirable goods because all the money is now in Advanistan. By degrees it becomes almost impossible for the people of Backwardistan to pay for these products, no matter how desirable they are because in local terms the prices for these products are skyrocketing in cost.

At the same time the primitive products that Backwardistan produces have become absurdly cheap because there is no gold left in the country. All the gold has been exported to Advanistan. An ounce of gold can now buy a ton of stuff. The gold supply of Advanistan is exploding because of its favorable balance of trade with its new trading partner and with its newly acquired wealth; it now discovers that their primitive trading partner has cheap and exotic trade goods to offer. Their tropical mahogany forests are now yielding tons of wonderfully carved mahogany statues, furniture, bowls, and plates that can be acquired for almost nothing. Ostrich feathers and parrots become wildly popular and then emeralds are discovered. It is now a whole new ballgame and gold begins to flood back into Backwardistan. The trade between the partners is now in balance and each country can now purchase the highly desirable products that the other has to offer. A win-win scenario has been created and there are no losers, only winners.

The thought experiment is over with and it is now obvious that the United States can't have had 40 years with an unfavorable balance of trade no matter how backward it might be. Mercantilism, and Mercantilism alone, explains the international economy and it is heading for a collapse. The question that must now be answered is how is it possible for this basically unsound system to survive for decades? And how can we profit from it?

If we ask: what went wrong? The answer is that we abolished the gold standard. The gold standard was the balancing scale that guaranteed that at the end of the day trade between nations would balance out, and that there would be no losers. The gold standard was replaced with the fiat money standard. Fiat money is money that is backed by nothing more than the full faith and credit of the nation that issues it. And therefore, unlike gold and silver, it can be printed in unlimited amounts. Without the gold standard there was nothing to keep the nations of the earth honest. They quickly discovered that under a fiat money system they could perpetually suppress the value of their currency below its market value, and by so doing export their unemployment to their trading partners and, over a series of years, gradually destroy the industrial base of their trading partners. The classic example of this is what Japan and China have done to the industrial base of the United States. They have virtually destroyed it.

How you suppress a currency below its market value for decades is a very complex matter even if you have a background in economics. There are three components to this process. The only component that you ever hear about is the special rules and regulations that countries erect to protect politically powerful sectors of their economy, like the farmers. Far more important is the second component, which is the manipulation your interest rates to insure that they are below those of your target country. By lowering your interest rates you tend to weaken the value of your currency. Consider this, at the time this is being written, the Fed funds rate for the United States is 5.25%, but for Japan it is 0%. That is right: zero. And it has been zero since it started its notorious ZIRP (zero interest rate policy) in 1996. As these words are being written, Japan has finally broken down and raised its rate to 0.25%.

There is, however, a more complex and much more powerful method that can be used even if your interest rates are above those of your target nation, you simply buy the treasury bonds of your target nation. Here is how it works, imagine that Toyota earns a profit of say $100 million selling cars in the states. When the headquarters in Tokyo receive the dollars, they present the dollars to Japan's central bank to exchange them for yen. At this point the bank of Japan creates the yen to purchase these dollars out of thin air. The important point to remember here is that Japan has created $100 million more yen than their national policy feels comfortable with and this has some inflationary consequences, and it can have a great deal of inflationary impact if you are generating a huge trade surplus. There is of course a way around this; it is called sanitizing the trade surplus. Japan can issue $100 million in bonds to sop up this surplus. The problem with this is that now it has created more debt than it wants. As a general rule most nations don't sanitize their foreign trade surpluses because it is too expensive. This is an important point to remember when we consider the case for gold.

Having received the $100 million the bank of Japan immediately uses the dollars to purchase U.S. treasury bonds. Purchasing these bonds has a profound impact. It short circuits the fact that Japan has a huge trade surplus with the United States and enables Japan to suppress the value of the yen below its market value. In other words, no matter how huge Japan's trade surplus is with the United States, the value of the yen will never rise as long as it uses its trade surplus to purchase U.S. Treasuries and therefore its trade with the United States will never balance. In other words again, when the central bank of any nation buys the treasury bonds or securities of the United States, it has the same effect as if they were buying our cars or toothpaste.

Before this is over, the world will feel the wrath of Adam Smith. We have created a world in which there is one bag holder, the United States, and it is bailing out the rest of the world.

The latest GDP (gross domestic product) of the United States is about $12.5 trillion and our trade deficit is a staggering 7% of our GDP. The world has never witnessed anything like it. The rule of thumb is that countries go into financial crisis whenever the trade deficit exceeds 5%. The only reason that the whole financial order hasn't blown up is that the dollar is the world's reserve currency.

In the world of Adam Smith foreign trade had an important but subordinate role to the domestic economy. No one ever contemplated a world in which the prosperity of all economies would be export-driven. This world was only born in the 1950's when Japan discovered to its considerable surprise that the United States was stupid enough to open up its economy to such an extent that it would result in the wholesale destruction of its industrial base, while Japan flatly refused to open up its highly protected domestic economy. As Japan proved how powerful an export-driven economy could be, the rest of the world took notice and followed in Japan's footsteps with Asia in the lead. The age of Asian Mercantilism had begun. The Asian nations would export their way to prosperity while keeping their own domestic economies protected. The rest of the world placed strict limits on how much trade abuse they would tolerate, to everyone's amazement the United States did not.

China is the straw that will break the camel's back. The skyrocketing prices of gold, silver, and the entire natural resource complex may be a warning that the final days are arriving. It will probably start with gold, which has always been the best barometer of the world's financial condition. Some Asian central banker who is contemplating the ever growing mountain of dollars in his vault that he knows has an ever declining real worth will decide to swap them for gold and the avalanche will begin. The skyrocketing price of gold may be an indicator that this is already happening. The collapse of the dollar will have a profound impact on the world economy. Since gold and all natural resources and commodities are priced in dollars, a dollar collapse will send all natural resources through the roof.

THE RISE OF THE PHOENIX

The phoenix is a mythological bird that consumed itself by fire and rose reborn from its ashes. The collapse of the dollar may be just what is needed to supercharge the American economy. Beneath the surface America is a very competitive economy. To a remarkable extent it is an economy with very few weaknesses. Since the end of the Second World War every nation on earth has sent its national champions to the brutal bloodstained gladiatorial arena that is the richest prize and most open market on earth. The competition has been brutal. An endless succession of foreign national champions and American companies have had their mangled, broken bodies dragged out of this bloodstained arena feet first. Those American companies that survived the bloodbath are beneath the surface far more competitive than is realized. America is Adam Smith's most loyal child, born under the star of capitalism in the very year that *The Wealth Of Nations* was published. It has always been more willing than most nations to accept Adam Smith's brutal dictum that all who can't compete must perish. And perish, they have, an endless succession of labor unions and companies have been mowed down without pity. What remains is the most flexible and adaptable labor force on earth. When the dollar collapses, the rest of the world will hear from us. And it will feel the wrath of Adam Smith.

The basis of capitalism is that markets are smarter than politicians and bureaucrats. If the reverse were true, then the communist countries would have the most successful economies on earth and then would come the socialist nations in second place, and the capitalist nations would have the lowest standard of living on earth. Bureaucrats and politicians will never be smarter than the market. The Asian Mercantilist nations have assumed that their politicians and bureaucrats are smarter than the market. They have built a Mercantilist house of cards based on this assumption and when it blows up, their economies are going to be put through the wringer.

Let's now take a look at the consequences of the Asian Mercantilist export model, which results in an export sector that is dangerously overdeveloped, deformed really in relation to their domestic economy. Since the United States is the bag holder for the world, what Asia is doing in effect is lending the United States the money to buy its products. When the dollar collapses, it will be revealed that these industries were built to serve a market that can't exist in the long run. Is it possible that they could redirect their exports to other nations? To a very limited extent yes, but no other nation will tolerate the wholesale destruction of their domestic industries the way the United States did. Well then what about redeploying their export industries to serve the domestic market? The problem with this is that the domestic market may already be served. In addition you have to ask yourself how much demand would there be to purchase the giant refrigerators, TV's, central air conditioners, and a host of other very expensive items from Asians. Many of whom live in dwellings that are so small that they couldn't even find the space to place these items even if they could afford them. Not to mention the electricity to run them.

Now the first five years after the dollar collapses will probably be an ugly time for everyone because the whole international system will be in upheaval. The export-driven

Asian economies will run into a ditch, but things will be very different for the United States. The collapse of the dollar will make foreign products too expensive to buy and domestic products will be dirt cheap in comparison. This will ignite an enormous economic boom in the United States as domestic industries expand to capture the 7% of the GDP that was served by foreign imports, but it won't stop there, the United States, freed from the shackles of a prohibitively priced dollar, could will become a fire breathing exporting juggernaut.

The Mercantilist nations won't take lightly the loss of the all-important American market and they will fight savagely to protect their market position. They will adopt a series of measures to debase their currencies relationship to the dollar, which will cause inflation to soar. A series of competitive worldwide devaluations among the Mercantilist nations is a real possibility. In such a world, the prices of all natural resources will go through the roof, and gold will lead the charge. The price of gold could reach truly amazing levels if this occurs.

CASE STUDY GOLD

The first thing you have to know about gold is that gold has always been about jewelry and only secondarily about the gold standard and investments. Indeed, until the huge gold discoveries of the 19th century there wasn't even enough gold in existence to serve as a money supply. Today, in a typical year, about 75% to 80% of all the gold that is consumed is used for jewelry. For the more inclusive time period of 1981 to 2005 78% of all gold produced was used for jewelry. Coins, gold bars, and industrial uses make up the rest. The second thing you have to know is its incredible rarity. Today, it isn't unusual for a gold mine to have to process ten tons of ore to retrieve a single ounce of gold. And there are mines where the grade is far lower than that. The entire world's gold supply is the equivalent of about two thirds of an ounce of gold for every human being and about 20% of this supply is held in the vaults of the central banks of the world.

In 1980 the world's gold production was about 1,200 tons, in that year gold reached its all-time high of $850 an ounce. Gold had been in a raging bull market for most of the 1970's, during this time it had risen 24 times in value from its historic fixed price of $35 an ounce to $850 an ounce. During this period huge fortunes were made by those who bought and held the precious metal.

It goes without saying that the most dazzling performers of all were gold penny mining stocks. Indeed the performance of the most spectacular penny mining stocks is hard to credit. I have an Internet report from Stanberry and Associates which gives the performance figures for some of the champion performers during the great gold bull market.

International Corona Resources up 5,445%
Goliath Gold up 7,011%
Golden Scepter up 7,650%
Consolidated Stikine up 73,010%

Then something happened that the gold bugs couldn't believe was possible. The central banks of the United States, the Common Market, and Japan got together and agreed to pop the great inflationary bubble that had been born in the 1970's and had propelled the great bull market in gold, silver and commodities. In the 1977-1981 period the consumer price index had risen a horrific 12.6% annually signaling runaway inflation. By 1980, during the height of the Carter-era economy, the rate continued to accelerate to a ghastly inflation rate of 14%. During this time I remember mortgage rates in the 14%-16% range. In the United States the central bank charge was led by Fed chairman Paul Volcker, who with incredible courage raised short-term interest rates to 21% and in so doing broke the back of inflation. What followed was a brutal bear market in gold that didn't end until 1999 when gold fell to a price of $253 an ounce and then began its long relentless climb to today's $630 an ounce.

The anti-gold forces point to gold's brutal 19-year bear market as proof that it is a barbarous relic and that gold has lost its historic anti-inflation role. After all, they say, inflation continued after 1980 even if it did so at a considerably reduced rate while gold simply collapsed. As we will see, the facts are more complex than that. I will start by saying that unlike the oil industry, the law of supply and demand worked with ruthless efficiency in the gold market. The 24-fold increase in the price of gold caused worldwide demand for gold to implode. The fabrication of new gold jewelry almost came to a complete stop in the first two years after 1980, and it was years before it recovered, but while the demand for gold was disintegrating, the production of gold was exploding from 1980's 1,200 tons to 2,700 tons in 2000. Since the year 2000 gold production has stabilized. In the year 2006, gold production declined and it is expected to flat line for the next year or two before production slowly increases over the following few years.

Everywhere you look today in the world of commodities you see a constant struggle just to maintain current production let alone increase it. In the world of natural resources, depletion is an unrelenting force while the barriers to bringing on new production increase with every year. The world is ignoring, to its considerable peril, the impact of ever-increasing government regulations and the growing army of lawyers that the Greens command, and their power to kill new mining proposals, which in many historic mining areas is now nearly absolute.

Just consider the historic mining states of California and Colorado. In a rational world this is one of the first places in North America that you would look for to find new mines. Forget it! As far as I am aware no new mine has gone into production in either state in the last 20 years, and the chance of any future mines going into production are about zero. These states have some of the most punitive anti-mining legislation on the books that exist and behind them is an inexhaustible army of green lawyers to back them up.

When people make their mindless assumptions about increasing prices resulting in increasing production they do so in total ignorance of these facts. An astonishing fact that only a careful reading of the Northern Miner will reveal is the amazing rise of green power in the third world and its surprising ability to block new mining projects. This is most evident in Latin America, where the greens have proven to be masters at praying on the fears of the peasants and nationalistic groups.

Consider what is arguably the world's greatest mineral treasure house, the Andes Mountain region of South America.

Just recently the nations of Bolivia, Peru, and Venezuela have repudiated existing legislation and passed new punitive anti-natural resource legislation. The rest of the third world has been taking notes. Nigeria and Outer Mongolia are two of many other resource rich nations that have recently introduced punishing new oil and mining laws.

Even more important, gold seems to be in a permanent deficit position. World production is about 2,700 tons, but world demand is about 3,800 tons per year. This deficit is made up by above ground sales, primarily central bank sales and recycled gold jewelry and gold coins. What is of great interest about this is that the world thinks that investment demand drives the price of gold, where in reality investment demand was until the last two years very minor. In 1996 investment demand was only 7% of jewelry demand, and by the year 2000 it was almost negative.

I recently read an interesting report on the Internet by a major coin dealer who was around for the 1980 gold boom. He said that for 24 years after 1980, he received an unrelenting supply of gold coins and gold bars that had been brought in by investors who had given up on gold. These coins and bars were then melted down and converted into jewelry. He reported that it was only in recent months that he has seen real investment demand reappear. And it is investment demand that is the great swing driver for gold. It is what drove gold in the last great bull market from $35 an ounce to $850 an ounce. Jewelry provides the stable base of gold demand.

Six thousand years of history proves that gold is an inflation hedge, but it is obvious that the law of supply and demand and its use in jewelry supersedes its role as an inflation hedge. The next chapter in the history of gold will be written in Asia and not in the West. It is India and China that will call the tune, 15 years ago gold consumption in China and India was negligible, today it is huge and growing. The three largest consumers of gold are India followed by America and China. Gold demand in India rose 47% last year and by 14% in China, where it is still partially regulated. In the year 2005 India surpassed Italy as the world's leading producer of gold jewelry. A title Italy had held for many years. Gold is what economists call a superior good, the wealthier you become, the more you consume. India last year consumed a remarkable 23% of the world's gold production, 95% of that amount is used for jewelry and 50% to 75% of this amount is bought for weddings. In the 1990's as India boomed, its gold demand increased by an amazing four times. Rumor has it that thanks to India's growing prosperity, these blushing darlings are so weighed down with gold that they can hardly move and they are forced to arrive at the festivities on a forklift.

There are three themes that could result in gold skyrocketing past its $850 an ounce high. The first is the collapse of the dollar. The second is a severe reduction in central bank gold sales. And the third is if Asian central banks decide to convert some of their massive dollar hoards into gold.

Since annual gold production doesn't come close to meeting annual gold consumption, everything depends on the remaining "above ground" supply. A supply the dimensions of which can only be guessed at, but that is shrinking each year. In the end the willingness of the central banks to keep dumping their ever-shrinking gold supplies into the market will be decisive. Few people realize how decisive central bank sales are in determining the price of gold. Since 1965 central banks have been consistent net sellers of gold, in the last 16 years they have averaged 14 million ounces a year in sales. It is highly doubtful that this pace can be maintained much longer. Many of the chronic gold sellers are now out of business forever. Simply put, they have no more gold to sell and other sellers are reaching the point where they will resist any further sales from their seriously depleted vaults. The day of decision will arrive when some Asian central banker decides to buy gold with their ever-growing mountain of dollars instead of U.S. treasuries. And the prime candidate for this is China, as this is being written China has just surpassed Japan as the world's greatest holder of U.S. treasury bonds. China's, massive foreign exchange reserves are 70% in U.S. treasury bonds and only 1% of its reserves are in gold.

U.S. PAPER MONEY TO GOLD RATIO FORT KNOX

1945 - 1.21 : 1
1968 - 3.97 : 1
2006 - 70.85 : 1

Study the above statistics; they indicate an ever-growing mountain of paper dollars in circulation in relation to the world's greatest hoard of gold. This process in the end must result in a vastly higher gold price. As of March 2006 the total value of the entire world's known gold was about $2.7 trillion. The total value of the entire U.S. stock and bond markets was $35 trillion. If investors diverted even 1% of this amount into gold, that amount would equal eight times the world's annual gold production. And this figure ignores the value of the rest of the world's stock and bond markets.

What the world has witnessed since the end of the Second World War as the above figures indicate is the creation of mountains of new paper money. And believe it or not the United States has been one of the most responsible nations.

The first paper currency was invented in China in the 13th century. Marco Polo reported on it in amazement. It was only accepted because the refusal to accept it was punishable by death. Since that time every paper currency ever created has ended up with a zero value. There aren't any exceptions to this. None! The only question has always been how many generations it will take you to get to zero. It is hard to credit what absolute garbage most of the world's currencies are. The three soundest currencies the world has ever known are the British pound, the U.S. dollar, and the Swiss franc. Aside from these there are amazingly few currencies in the world that a prudent investor would regard as being even remotely sound. And none of the world's currencies can be considered totally sound. And don't prattle nonsense to me about the German mark. How long did that last? The truth of the matter is that twice in the 20th Century the German mark became worthless. The British pound was once worth one pound of silver and $20 dollars used to be worth on ounce of gold.

What the anti-gold forces fail to realize when they trot out their old shopworn arguments against gold is that year after year the situation is shifting more and more in gold's favor. Every nation has printing presses that are out of control. Every developed nation and surprising numbers of third-world nations have promised their citizens benefits that they can't deliver on without resorting to massive inflation. The day of retribution is coming and those who are smart enough to bet on gold will be handsomely rewarded.

CASE STUDY SILVER

My interest in silver goes back a very long way indeed. I still have in my possession a booklet on silver written in 1969 by C.V. Myers, the godfather of the silver bulls. Myers began beating the drum on silver when the maximum allowable price for silver was still fixed by the government at $1.29 per ounce. I will never forget when Myers told his followers that the time had come to sell silver. He said something like this: "I know that I have predicted much higher prices than $5.00 an ounce, but it just hasn't materialized and under the circumstances I recommend that you sell silver at $5.00 an ounce." This was only a couple of months before silver started its rocket ride to $50 an ounce.

The interesting thing about the silver bulls is that they are all gold bugs who happen to believe that silver is a better investment than gold, and they have strong reasons for believing this to be true. It is hard to know where to begin talking about this truly amazing metal. It is a precious metal that in the 20th Century became an industrial metal without the world realizing it. Until about 100 years ago silver was just like gold, it had no industrial uses with the notable exception of photography. Its traditional uses were the same as gold. It was used as jewelry, coinage, and investment bars. Then suddenly its industrial uses exploded. New discoveries in industry led to an ever-growing consumption of silver for photography, light and heat transfer electronics, catalysts, and medicine. The fact that silver is the best conductor of electricity known has tremendous significance. In these 100 years these new industrial uses of silver have consumed the cumulative silver production of thousands of years.

For several centuries the historic relationship between gold and silver was 15 to 16 ounces of silver were equal in value to one ounce of gold. Then in the 19th Century and the early part of the 20th Century the vast silver deposits of the Comstock lode in

Virginia City, Nevada and the Coeur d'Alene deposits in Idaho were discovered and the price of silver collapsed. The maximum allowable price of silver was then fixed by the government at $1.29 an ounce until the great gold & silver bull markets of the 1970's. At the moment this is being written the relationship between gold and silver is 49 ounces of silver equals one ounce of gold. At its worst, the ratio was 80 to one.

According to a recent Internet study done by silver bull David Zurbuchen, since the beginning of recorded history, a total of about 44.55 billion ounces of silver have been produced and about 4.25 billion ounces of gold for a ratio of 10.5 to one. Currently about 32% of silver is used in jewelry about 25% in photography and 40% for industrial uses. If you consider photography an industrial use, which it is, you are at 65% industrial. Only about 30% of the world's annual production of silver comes from pure silver mines, the remaining silver production is as a byproduct from base metal mines, primarily lead and zinc mines. For most of the time period since the 1980 crash in gold and silver the price of silver has fluctuated between $4.00 and $6.00 an ounce. At this price it is almost impossible to find mines with ores rich enough to turn a profit, most silver mines have struggled just to stay open and it has been very difficult to find operational silver mines that were worth investing in. This is the reason why 70% of the world's silver production comes as a byproduct from base metal mining. Pure silver mines for the most part couldn't survive.

There is one more technical point about silver production that needs to be discussed, silver is created by a process called "epithermal deposition". Which means that most silver is deposited near the earth's surface and the deeper you dig the poorer the ore body becomes. For other metals the opposite is true, the deeper you dig the richer the ore becomes. This doesn't bode well for future discoveries. In the last two years, however, the price of silver has skyrocketed to above $12 an ounce; at this price it is a whole new ballgame for the pure silver producers.

Then there is the silver deficit, every year since 1990 more silver has been consumed than is produced, as has been the case in gold the balance has been made up from "above ground" stocks, which are rapidly depleting. According to the latest

Silver Year Book from 1990 to 2005 the accumulated net silver deficit was around 1.96 billion ounces. In the silver market as in the gold market everything depends on how large the above ground stocks are, and no one can know for sure. The issue is where do you place your bets.

In 1959 the U.S. treasury possessed the greatest hoard of silver the world had ever known, a massive 2.06 billion ounces of silver. In the year 2002 the U.S. treasury announced that it had exhausted its once vast silver hoard and would now be forced to buy silver on the open market to supply its annual sales of its popular commemorative silver coins and silver eagle bullion coins. Recently the silver eagle bullion sales have averaged about 10.5 million ounces a year.

The silver bull's most critical insight is that it is estimated that about 85% to 90% of the 4.25 billion ounces of gold that has ever been produced is today readily available. Obviously all these figures must be taken with more than a few grains of salt and the sources are rarely in complete agreement.

Readily available gold exists in the form of jewelry, gold coins, and in central banks in the form of gold bars. Silver today however has mutated into primarily an industrial metal without the world becoming aware of it. It is now being consumed for thousands of industrial uses almost always in very small amounts and therefore can't readily be reclaimed.

In addition to the uses already touched upon, silver's superiority as a conductor of electricity has resulted in it being used in very small amounts primarily for contact points on thousands of electrical systems. All electroplating contains silver. All our solar energy systems and water purification systems contain silver. The electrical batteries used to power our watches; cell phones etc. all contain silver. The typical washing machine uses about 15 to 20 silver coated switches. Every auto produced in America has silver-ceramic lines fired into the rear window to clear away frost and ice. Silver is the most efficient reflector of light; all of our mirrors contain silver. It goes on and on. Those wishing to peruse the thousands of industrial uses for silver can look it up on the Silver Institutes's website.

Too much has been made of the coming demise of silver in photography. After messing around with digital photography, I for one feel that the advantages have been greatly overstated. It is important to realize that a great deal of silver will still be consumed in photography in the form of glossy photos, all of which consume silver halides and in medical x-rays. Photography will be a massive, if declining, consumer of silver for decades to come.

We have now arrived at the core of the silver bulls argument. Let's assume that about 85% of all the gold ever produced is readily available (we must beware of any attempt at too much false precision with these numbers). That leaves us with about 3.6 billion ounces of readily available gold. According to the Silver Institute because of the relentless draw down of silver inventories since 1990, there are only about 670 million ounces of readily available silver that is known to exist. The largest of these supplies is the 120 million ounces held at the COMEX warehouses. The annual silver deficit draw down fluctuates widely from as low as 40 to 50 million ounces in recessions to as high as 200 million ounces in boom years. These are shocking figures if they are even close to being true. It means that there is more readily available gold than there is silver in the world.

One doesn't have to be a Sherlock Holmes to figure out what the argument of the naysayers is. They say that these figures are nuts and that demand will create its own supply, that there are vast unknown supplies in India and elsewhere that will flood the market when the price of silver rises, and to a certain extent they are right. I have vivid memories of the last silver bull market when silver went up in value 38 times. People were lined up in front of coin dealers three times around the block with their junk silver to cash in. The question is how much junk silver is still left? How much junk silver do you own? How much junk silver do your friends own? Ask around.

My very unscientific survey says that there is very little junk silver left, people are clueless about why anyone in his or her right mind would want to own gold or silver. Every time I bring up the subject of my two favorite metals, everyone sits around and gawks at me. In the 19th century Americans were the most gold crazed people on earth. Today Americans are clueless as to why anyone in his or her right mind would want to own gold or silver. In the Western world gold and silver have virtually been eliminated as an investment category. If people were ever to decide to put as little as 1% of their investment capital into gold and silver, the price of both metals would go to prices that are inconceivable. As a coin collector I will maintain a discreet silence about how much junk silver I own. Coin World had a recent article about this matter; they quoted David Hendrickson of Silvertowne, one of the largest silver dealers in the country. He stated: "There aren't hundreds of bags of 90% silver coins coming in like there were in 1980."

The conventional thesis is that we live in a world of unending natural resource abundance. I think the world is in for an ugly shock. The age of natural resource abundance is dying and the age of natural resource scarcity is being born. As I have already stated, there is no profit in betting that tomorrow is going to be like today, but there are huge profits to be made betting that tomorrow will be different than today. If I am right, huge profits will be made by betting on "wealth in the ground", but if I am wrong, my losses will be minor.

LAYING MY CARDS ON THE TABLE

Writing this book has been a revelation to me. It has forced me to think through opinions that I had long believed in and analyze them down to the bottom, and by doing so crystallize them and bring them to the surface. The most astonishing thing that it taught me was that I was a riverboat gambler and never knew it. I had always regarded myself as a pretty conservative person. I could never figure out why I could never talk friends and family into investing in what they regarded as my weirdo investments, but they seemed perfectly reasonable to me. After all, I had researched them, and in many cases I had been following them for more than 30 years.

A splendid little company like Cream Minerals at 23 cents a share seemed like a great deal to me. They thought I was nuts. I knew that it was part of the Frank Lang Group. Its principal property was the Kaslo silver property with 9,600 acres in British Columbia. This property encompassed nine former silver producers, the last of which had closed down in 1966. It had opportunity written all over it if you were a riverboat gambler. If you weren't a riverboat gambler you could never get past the fact that it was selling at 23 cents a share and hadn't been a producer since 1966.

The whole point of all this has been to welcome you to my world, a strange and wondrous world where fabulous returns are available for chump change investments. A world where you can become a riverboat gambler and never have to face the threat of financial ruin. Who couldn't learn to love such a world? What more could anyone ask for? It is now time for a detailed analysis of my positions.

MUTUAL FUNDS

MATTHEWS ASIAN GROWTH AND INCOME $17.94
PIMCO COMMODITY REAL RETURN FUND $14.28
T.R.PRICE EMERGING MARKETS BOND FUND $12.99

In addition to the above mutual funds, I also own the Korean Equity Mutual Fund and the New Ireland Mutual Fund, both of which I will probably be selling in the near future. It will be observed that with the exception of the Pimco Commodity fund, all my mutual funds are overseas investments. It is important that everyone has an exposure to foreign investments and mutual funds are the best way of achieving this requirement. The Pimco Commodity fund is a rare breed of cat that invests in commodities and is therefore worth your careful consideration.

REITS

FIRST INDUSTRIAL REALTY TRUST (7.5%) $38.09
GLENBOROUGH REALTY TRUST (5.2%) $21.50
HEALTH CARE PROPERTY INVESTORS (6.6%) $26.68
HEALTHCARE REALTY TRUST (8.4%) $32.77
HRPT TRUST (7.5%) $11.39
MONMOUTH R. E. INVEST. CORP (7.6%) $8.09
NATIONAL RETAIL PROPERTIES (6.8%) $19.89
NEW PLAN EXCEL REALTY TRUST (5.2%) $24.74
PLUM CREEK TIMBER COMPANY (4.6%) $35.70
RAYONIER INC. (5.2%) $37.26
SOVRAN SELF STORAGE (5.1%) $51.12
SUN COMMUNITIES (8.1%) $32.45
TRUSTREET PROPERTIES (10.2%) $13.08
UNITED MOBILE HOMES (6.5%) $15.27

Real Estate Investment Trusts are an absolute must. They are the core holdings of my income portfolio. The yields of course aren't what they used to be now that they have been discovered, but they are still pretty impressive.

First Industrial Realty Trust and Monmouth Real Estate Investment Corp. comprise the industrial REITs. First Industrial is the largest industrial REIT in the United States.

Glenborough Realty Trust is an office REIT that specializes in high-quality multi-tenant office buildings and currently owns 48 office properties.

Health Care Property Investors is an REIT that invests in hospitals and medical office buildings and currently has property interests in 527 properties in 42 states.

Healthcare Realty Trust is another hospital REIT that invests in and manages medical office properties and clinics. It currently manages 138 properties of which it owns 104.

HRPT Properties Trust is a REIT that specializes in office

buildings in which a large concentration of its office space is leased to the U.S. Government and medical tenants. It owns approximately 55 million square feet of office space in 32 states.

National Retail Properties has an interesting twist; it specializes in long-term triple net leases to single tenant properties often in the form of long-term sale-leasebacks. Typical clients are Barnes & Noble Booksellers, The Sports Authority and Best Buy. This results in an unusually reliable long-term income stream. They currently own 524 properties.

New Plan Excel Realty Trust is the Goliath of malls. It owns 476 properties, many of which are malls with a total leaseable space of 67 million square feet.

Plum Creek Timber Company- This unique must own REIT is a timberlands owning REIT. It owns a staggering 8.2 million acres of prime timberlands. It is interesting to note that its carefully selected fast-growing trees grow at an amazing 7% a year. Regrettably the stock market has discovered this REIT and as a result its dividend yield isn't what it used to be. If there is such a thing as a buy it and forget it stock, then Plum Creek is that stock.

Rayonier Inc.- This Plum Creek wannabe is the seventh largest private landowner in the country and the second largest timberland REIT, it owns 2.5 million acres of timberlands. Its specialty is as the premier supplier of high-value specialty cellulose fibers.

Sovran Self Storage is a self-storage provider operating under the Uncle Bob's brand. It owns 285 properties with a total of 150,666 rental spaces.

Sun Communities is an REIT that specializes in owning high quality mobile home parks. It owns 135 mobile home parks with a total of 47,300 home sites.

United Mobile Homes is a smaller version of Sun

Communities, it owns 27 mobile home communities with a total of 6,400 home sites.

Trustreet Properties is the largest REIT that services the restaurant industry largely through the use of long-term sale-leasebacks. It owns more than 2,000 restaurant properties. Major clients are Applebee's, Arby's, Burger King, Denny's, Pizza Hut and Wendy's.

OIL & GAS ROYALTY TRUSTS

CROSS TIMBERS ROYALTY (5.7%) $44.99
HUGOTON ROYALTY TRUST (6.9%) $25.17
PERMIAN BASIN ROYALTY TRUST (7.7%) $15.70
SABINE ROYALTY TRUST (8.2%) $42.76
SAN JUAN BASIN ROYALTY TRUST (6.6%) $33.32

I don't currently own Cross Timbers Royalty, but I am watching it.

Hugoton Royalty Trust has 15 years of proven reserves, which is huge in today's world, the typical oil firm struggles to maintain 8 to 10 years of proven reserves. Its royalties cover 407,000 acres and its production is 94% natural gas and 6% oil.

Permian Basin Royalty Trust covers 303,000 acres located in 33 counties in Texas. Permian Basin is unique in this group in the respect that more than 50% of its income comes from oil. For the rest of the group, natural gas is the primary income source.

Sabine Royalty Trust has 2,092,292 acres of royalty properties grouped into 5,400 tracts of land spread over the states of Florida, Louisiana, Mississippi, New Mexico, Oklahoma and Texas. Production is about 61% natural gas and 39% oil. The interesting thing about these royalty companies is that they always seem to discover more oil and gas than the geologists suspected was there. In its most recent annual report Sabine stated the following:

In 1982 when the trust was first formed, it was

estimated that the reserves for the trust were approximately 9 million barrels of oil and 62 billion cubic feet of gas. At the time the trust was expected to have a life span of 9 or 10 years and be fully depleted by 1993. In the 24 years since the inception, the trust has produced approximately 16 million barrels of oil and 210 billion cubic feet of gas. With this year's reserve estimate of 6.3 million barrels of oil and 36.4 billion cubic feet of gas remaining, it could be estimated that the trust still has a life span of 8 to 10 years. The current economic conditions create an environment that could further expand and enhance the distributions in the years to come.

San Juan Basin Royalty Trust's properties cover 151,900 acres in northwest New Mexico's fabulous San Juan Basin. Which is one of the richest natural gas basins in the country. Production is about 97% natural gas and 3% oil.

I think you can see why royalty companies with their amazing dividends are one of my favorite investments. However, you need to be aware of the many phony baloney royalty companies that are out there. These companies were set up by their grantor's with "take back" provisions. One type of "take back" is that the royalty reverts back to the grantor after a term of years. The other "take back" is that after a predetermined period of years, the royalty holders receive a declining percentage of the royalty payments every year. Have nothing to do with these toxic scams.

CANADIAN INCOME TRUSTS

ARC ENERGY TRUST (10.4%) $19.39
BAXTEX ENERGY TRUST (10.7%) $16.96
FORDING CANADIAN COAL (14.6%) $22.68
HARVEST ENERGY TRUST (17.5%) $21.93
PENGROWTH ENERGY TRUST (14.9%) $16.91
PENWEST ENERGY ENERGY TRUST (11.4%) $30.05
PRIMEWEST ENERGY TRUST (13.3%) $19.15
THUNDER ENERGY TRUST (25.6%) $4.77

As always it is the small, the obscure, and the unknown investments that produce the greatest rewards. Just check out the yields of this relatively unknown investment category. These trusts are set up so that the trust pays no taxes because all income flows through to the shareholder.

Arc Energy Trust's landholdings are concentrated in the Canadian province of Alberta. Its income is split about 50-50 between natural gas and oil. It also has a conservative payout ratio of about 59%.

Baxtex Energy Trust operates primarily in western Canada. Its production is about 70% oil and 30% natural gas. Its payout ratio is a conservative 53%. Its production is about 70% oil and about 30% natural gas. About 83% of its oil production is heavy oil.

Fording Canadian Coal Trust has a PE ratio of 5.3 and has a 60% ownership in the Elk Valley coal partnership in British Columbia. This is the second largest exporter of high-quality metallurgical coal needed for the manufacture of steel in the world.

Harvest Energy Trust- I never purchased this company. I was the happy owner of Viking Energy Trust, a smaller outfit that paid a 18% dividend and was merged into Harvest. As a result of the merger I have a smaller dividend, but I own a considerably larger outfit. Harvest's production is 75% oil and 25% natural gas. I of course voted against the merger as I vote against almost all mergers. It almost never does me any good obviously. My fellow shareholders think it is wonderful that they are being bought out at a crummy 15% to 20% premium. I think it is an insult. While they are celebrating, I am crying. They are too stupid to know the value of their company. I am not. Nor is the shrewd competitor that is buying them out. Rest assured that if I thought the company was only worth 15% to 20% more than its purchase price, I would have never bought it. If you are a small-cap value player who knows what a bargain looks like, buyouts will be the bane of your existence. You will be living in a world in which your fellow shareholders think that their stock's intrinsic value is its current market price. Every time you turn around, some shrewd competitor will make some low-ball offer that your fellow shareholders will be deliriously happy to accept. Then you will be faced with the often-impossible task of finding a replacement for them that is just as good. At least that has been my experience. I have never been able to find good replacements for stocks like Koger Equity or my fabulous gold royalty company, Franco Nevada, that was stolen from me when Newmont Mines bought it out for peanuts.

As this is being written two of my stocks have buyout offers. In an act of unspeakable depravity Nova Gold is trying to takeover Pioneer Metals. The only thing different about this hostile takeover attempt is that instead of the usual insulting 15% to 20% premium, Nova Gold is offering a 30% premium. I am having none of it. I couldn't vote against this offer fast enough, and for once the whole board is opposed to the offer. As these words are being written the Nova Gold offer has just been trumped by a new offer from Barrick Gold at $1.00 a share. The Pioneer Metals board has recommended acceptance of this new offer. And so it goes in the world of the small-cap value investor.

Strangely enough I'm not opposed to the other offer. This is probably because I own both the acquiring company and the takeover target. Western Canadian Coal is merging with Northern Energy And Mining.

Pengrowth Energy Trust has land holdings throughout Canada and is a leader in coal bed methane extraction.

Penn West Energy Trust is Canada's largest energy trust. It has a 38% ownership in the immense long-life Pembina Cardium field, the largest conventional light oil pool ever found in Canada, which is located in Alberta. Penn West total oil reserves are estimated at 7.8 billion barrels and it has a low debt ratio. It has a 60% payout ratio and an enormous land inventory of almost five million acres.

PrimeWest Energy Trust's landholdings are 250,000 acres

concentrated in the province of Alberta. Its production is 75% natural gas and 25% oil. Its debt to capitalization ratio is only 10%. And it is becoming a growing factor in coal bed methane production.

Thunder Energy Trust has 692,000 acres of landholdings, primarily in Alberta. Its production is 63% natural gas and 37% oil. The payout ratio is about 65%. Thunder Energy is my smallest producer. In today's world this isn't a disadvantage. In a world in which every energy producer is struggling just to maintain production let alone increase it, the only thing Thunder has to do is pick up the telephone and its competitors will be lined up three times around the block to engage in a bidding war for its assets. In the meantime, I am being paid a 17% dividend.

MASTER LIMITED PARTNERSHIPS

DIANA SHIPPING LP (12.8%) $10.92
DORCHESTOR MINERALS (11.6%) $25.52
ENTERPRISE PARTNERS (7.1%) $25.08
MARTIN MIDSTREAM PT (7.9%) $31.07
NATIONAL RESOURCE PT (5.8%) $54.45
PLAINS ALL AMERICAN LP (6.5%) $43.77
U.S. SHIPPING PARTNERS (8.5%) $20.79

It will be observed by looking at the dividend yields that MLP's are another investment category that investors know nothing about.

Diana Shipping has a PE ratio of only 7.3 and specializes as a dry bulk carrier carrying such cargoes as iron ore, coal, and grains. It has a fleet of 14 ships of which 13 are Panamax, the largest ships that can transit the Panama Canal. The other ship is a cape size, too large to transit either the Panama or the Suez Canal. The age of the fleet is just under four years. It is felt that a fleet of this type has great operational flexibility since all but one of the ships can transit both the Panama and the Suez Canal.

Dorchester Minerals- This oil and gas producer has a PE

ratio of 12.7. It has total gross landholdings of 132,714 acres located in 573 counties in 25 states.

Enterprise Partners is one of the largest pipelines in the country. Its highly strategic pipelines transport oil and natural gas through 32,776 miles of both onshore and offshore pipelines, which penetrate deep into the Gulf of Mexico. Since Enterprise went public in July of 1998 it has increased its cash distributions 15 times by a total of 94%.

Martin Midstream Partners is a unique duck that is primarily engaged in river barge transportation of bulk commodities on the Mississippi river basin. It is also engaged in terminalling and storage of petroleum, sulfur, and fertilizer products.

National Resource Partners owns a staggering two billion tons of coal with a reserve life of approximately 38 years. National Resource wisely doesn't operate any mines. Rather it leases its vast coal reserves to mine operators under long-term leases in exchange for royalty payments. Its reserves are located in 11 states.

Plains All American Pipeline is another pipeline that keeps increasing its dividends. It has 15,000 miles of pipelines. It is also a sizable owner of 39 million barrels of crude oil storage facilities.

U.S. Shipping Partners is an intriguing outfit. It is a Jones Act shipping company that serves the U.S. coastwise trade. The Jones Act gives American shipping a monopoly in the so-called coastwise trade when shipping from one American port to another American port. U.S. Shipping is the largest Jones Act shipper in its specialty, which is the transportation of refined petroleum products and basic chemicals for major oil and chemical companies in its fleet of ten highly specialized tank vessels.

Fred Carach

CONVENTIONAL OIL & GAS COMPLEX

EMBER RESOURCES $2.41
GASCO ENERGY $2.32
GREY WOLF $6.80
PETROGEN .26
PETRO. DEVELOPMENT $37.72
SEITEL INC. $3.55
UTS ENERGY $3.71

Ember Resources- This is an interesting play on the growing importance of CBM (coal bed methane) as a new source of natural gas. The production of CBM in the United States has gone from almost nothing to 7% of total gas production in recent years. It is extracted by drilling into the coal seam where the gas is trapped as if it was an oil well. I acquired this stock as a result of a spin-off from Thunder Energy. Ember's mandate is to specialize in CBM production in the province of Alberta, where it owns 308,000 acres of highly prospective CBM lands.

Gasco Energy is a natural gas company that owns 264,000 acres in the Rocky Mountain play of Utah, Wyoming, and Nevada. It currently has 42 wells in production.

Grey Wolf is one of the leading contract land drillers in the United States and as you would expect its earnings are exploding. It owns 115 drilling rigs and has a PE of 10. I don't know what people are thinking of; at this price they are giving the stock away.

Petrogen- This is a very intriguing penny stock play. It owns two strategically located fields on the oil and gas rich Texas Gulf coast.

Petroleum Development Corp. is unusual, it operates about 2,800 wells, but its properties are primarily located in the east, in the Appalachian and Michigan basins. One of its primary profit drivers is its annual drilling partnership programs that it offers investors. I wish I had bought more of it when it was selling for

103

$5.90 a share.

Seitel Inc.- This is one of my favorite plays, the emerging from bankruptcy play. Seitel, a leading provider of seismic and geophysical data and services to the petroleum industry, emerged from bankruptcy in 2004. Its data library is immense. They own one of the largest, if not the largest, onshore data libraries in North America covering 35,000 square miles of 3D seismic data and 1.1 million linear miles of 2D seismic data which they rent out to interested parties. As they put it in their latest annual report: "when it comes to business strategy, we keep it simple. We license seismic data. So seismic data is what we invest in. We don't own field equipment or crews." when it emerged from bankruptcy in June of 2004, you could have bought it for $1.00. Not the least of its attractions is that it is still unknown. There are only 869 recorded stockholders.

UTS Energy is one of my most intriguing investments. It owns an interest in Canada's fabulous Athabasca oil sands play. It wisely farmed out 70% of its interest in the FT. Hills project to two majors, Petro-Canada and Teck, who have taken on the huge burden of developing the project, in return for which UTS Energy receives a free carried 30% interest. The FT. Hills project contains a staggering 2.8 billion barrels of oil. When it comes on stream, it will be producing at a rate of 190,000 barrels a day. In addition, UTS holds a 100% interest in 7,067 acres of nearby oil sands.

COAL & URANIUM

CANALASKA URANIUM .46
DENISON MINES $9.90
FOUNDATION COAL $34.10
HILLSBORO RESOURCES .45
INTERNATIONAL URANIUM $ 5.30
MESA URANIUM .50
PINE VALLEY MINING .15
STRATHMORE MINERALS $ 1.67
UEX CORPORATION $ 3.30
WESTERN CANADIAN COAL $ 1.30

Canalaska Uranium- Canada's Athabasca Basin is the world's richest uranium deposit and accounts for a third of global uranium production. Amazingly this penny mining stock has one of the largest portfolios of mining claims within the basin. A staggering 2,313,000 acres located in 18 separate parcels. Of course it must be realized that there is a huge difference between mining claims and proven reserves, but for 46 cents a share I am willing to take that risk.

As you will recall I am a raging bull on both coal and uranium. When I first discovered the uranium story, uranium was selling at about $18.00 a pound, today it is selling at $45.50 a pound and this move isn't over. The world's current supply of uranium is struggling to meet the needs of today's 442 nuclear power plants and there are currently 28 new plants under construction. If all of today's announced plants are built, the world's supply of nuclear power plants will increase to 506 plants in the next decade. Current world uranium production of 50,000 tons is now estimated at only about 62% of the world's 80,000-ton annual demand. The balance is being made up from declining above ground stocks. It doesn't get much better than this.

Denison Mines- This blue-chip holding is a producer with 15 million pounds of uranium reserves located in various uranium mining camps in North America. The most interesting thing it does is that the company acts as manager for the Uranium Participation Corporation, a publicly traded company that was created to invest in, hold, and sell uranium yellow cake. Its most important asset is its 22.5% junior interest in the McClean lake uranium mill located in the Athabasca basin and which is the third largest uranium mill in the world. This company is now profitable and debt free. As this is being written Denison Mines and International Uranium have announced that they are merging. If the proposed merger goes through, the new Denison Mines will become a North American uranium powerhouse. Each new Denison share will be worth 2.88 shares in the new Denison mines

Foundation Coal- This established blue-chip producer owns a diverse group of 13 mines with very impressive total proven reserves of 1.7 billion tons in the four great coal producing basins of the United States. The mines in the Northern and Central Appalachia Basin, the Illinois basin, and the ever more vital Powder River Basin provide an enviable mix of thermal coal to operate the nation's power plants and the high quality metallurgical coal required for steel production.

The most important takeaway is this; the United States is the Saudi Arabia of coal, our coal reserves, at 27% of total global reserves, are the greatest on earth. And at a high enough price these coal reserves can be converted into oil and natural gas. The process for converting coal into oil has been known since at least the Second World War when the Germans converted coal into oil to power their war machine. For the long-term investor who is willing to salt these coal stocks away and to think in terms of five to ten years, the rewards could be huge.

Hillsborough Resources- This intriguing penny mining stock has two producing mines. It is primarily a coal producer in British Columbia, the heartland of Canadian coal production and has just started its second mine in Tennessee. It has recently acquired metallurgical coal assets in British Columbia. The company is solidly profitable, which is unusual for a company selling for under a dollar.

International Uranium's primary asset is the 2,000-ton-per-day White Mesa uranium processing mill in Utah. It is one of only two such mills operating in the United States. It also owns a considerable portfolio of mining claims in the southwestern United States and in the all-important Athabasca Basin.

Mesa Uranium has a 100% interest in the Lisbon Valley project in southeast Utah that covers 27 square miles of uranium claims. This is one of my favorite plays, the ex-producer play.

The Lisbon mine was in production from 1972 to 1988 during which time it produced 22 million pounds of uranium. Mesa has two mining shafts and a processing mill that profitably produced uranium at an average price of $21.00 a pound. In total the Lisbon Valley district that Mesa now controls produced a total of 85 million pounds of uranium. The whole Lisbon Valley complex at its peak had 16 uranium mines that produced 103 million pounds of uranium. The astute reader will recall that uranium today is selling for $45.50 a pound. The last interesting fact about Mesa is that it has a stock float of only 18,585,000 shares outstanding. An amazingly small float in today's world. In other words at its current give away price of 50 cents a share, you could buy the whole company lock, stock, and barrel for an inexplicable $9,290,000.

Now I know what you are thinking. You are thinking: "Gee, Fred, how can the market be ignoring this type of value?" As these words are being written the entire coal and uranium complex is undergoing a brutal sell off across the board. The question is: why? Assuming that you can even find somebody on the Street who knows that coal and uranium stocks actually exist, and this could be a very big challenge, you will be informed that both coal and uranium have had some very nice moves over the last year or two, which is certainly true, and that their day in the sun is over. Therefore the wise investor will rotate out of these "has-been" stocks and buy into today's hot new investments. As I have already stated, stocks can be too good to be true if nobody knows that they exist. And these small, obscure, and unknown penny stocks can be estate builders if you just have the patience to hold on to them for five or ten years.

Pine Valley Mining- This is another classic British Columbia junior coal mining play. Their Willow Creek mine is now in production and metallurgical coal is being shipped by rail to Prince Rupert on the Pacific Ocean, and from there to clients in Asia. Production began in the autumn of 2005 and the company is modestly profitable. This is still a startup and there is a reasonable expectation of more lucrative profits in the future. In short a classic "wealth in the ground" play.

Strathmore Minerals is a very impressive junior uranium conglomerate. It has the largest land package in the critical Athabasca Basin; an amazing 2.8 million acres in mining claims or permit applications. It was an early convert to the coming uranium boom thesis and locked up an amazing amount of strategic land claims before the crowd arrived. It has an unusually strong land position in the New Mexico and Wyoming uranium districts. In addition, it has $20 million in working capital, an unusual amount for a stock selling for $1.67 a share.

UEX Corporation- I have already commented on this stock.

Western Canadian Coal- As I have already mentioned, this company is merging with another stock that I own, Northern Energy and Mining. The combined operation will have an impressive 85 million tons of proven coal reserves. The stock currently has one producing mine and two more mines are coming on-stream.

THE GOLD MINERS

BRALORNE GOLD MINES .79
CAMPBELL RESOURCES .14
CUSAC GOLD MINES .21
EXALL RESOURCES $ 1.85
GOLD CORP $27.22
KIRKLAND LAKE GOLD $ 6.46
KLONDEX GOLD $ 1.78
KLONDIKE GOLD .12
MONETA GOLD MINES .15
NEVADA PACIFIC $ 1.05
NORTHGATE MINERALS $ 3.19
PIONEER METALS .57
QUEENSTON MINING $ 1.06
RUBICON MINERALS $ .56
ST. ANDREWS GOLDFIELDS $ .95
TYHEE DEVELOPMENT .41
WHITE KNIGHT RESOURCES $ 1.64
X CAL RESOURCES .22

Now I know what you are thinking. You are thinking: "Gee, Fred, are you sure you own enough gold stocks?" Very funny! The most important thing about this list is that there is only one blue-chip gold stock on the list and that is Gold Corp. I don't own and can't recommend the other blue-chip golds because they are always overpriced and I think that they are going to have enormous problems just maintaining their gold production in the next few years. The second most important thing about this list is that in addition to Gold Corp there are only two other producers on the list and they are Kirkland Lake Gold and Northgate Minerals. By now you know my methods. The uninformed will simply dismiss these non-producers as a bunch of dubious penny mining stocks. I fondly regard them as my future moon shots. And you should too, fellow riverboat gamblers; these scorned penny mining stocks are the keys to the kingdom. If gold fluctuates around its current market value, then these stocks will more or less fluctuate with the price of gold. If however gold blasts past its old $850 an ounce, then these stocks can become 10 baggers and dare I say it 20 baggers. Since you never know which of these jewels lightning is going to strike next, you must throw a very wide net. Exall Resources is a classic example of an unexpected lightning strike that I was able to capitalize on only because I threw a very wide net. Two of the above stocks, Nevada Pacific Gold and White Knight Resources, won't be commented on by me, as it appears that they are about to be taken over by U.S. Gold. If they are, I will take the money and run.

Bralorne Gold Mines- This company is a consolidation of three ex-producers that from 1932 to 1971 produced 4.15 million ounces of gold. It is debt free and has a small float of 13,215,000 shares, at this price the whole operation is valued by the market at $10,440,000. It has an on site mill. Currently attempts are underway to bring the property into production.

Campbell Resources- I have already commented on this stock.

Cusac Gold Mines- This ex-producer owns several properties. Its prime property is its Table Mountain Mine, an 80-square-mile property with a 300-ton-per-day mill. It has a $20 million infrastructure and has been on a care and maintenance basis since 1999. It is currently attempting to get back into production. I have owned this stock since 1989 and somehow it hasn't been able to capitalize on its considerable assets, but the potential is there.

I am going to digress here and comment as to why my attitude toward penny mining stocks is so different from the all-prevailing popular opinion that all penny mining stocks are scams. It is indeed curious that almost never have these always-critical authorities owned a penny mining stock. And their ignorance about these stocks is monumental. I, on the other hand, have owned perhaps as many as 200 of these stocks since the 1960's and you know what, I can't recall ever being victimized by a scam. What does happen inevitably from time to time is that the CEO will "give up" on the company and just walk away. If that happens, the stock becomes worthless. Having said that, if you ever receive a phone call asking you to invest in a penny mining stock, hang up at once, it is indeed a scam. I never have and never will invest in such a company.

Cusac gold is an example of a CEO that stayed. Guilford H. Brett founded the company in 1965 and for 40 years he struggled with mixed success to turn the company into a producer. He retired in 2005 and turned the company over to his successor, David Brett, who has been with the company for more than 11 years. I think you will agree with me that this is a far cry from what people think penny mining stocks are all about.

Exall Resources- I have already commented on this stock.

Gold Corp.- This stock has come from nowhere in the last five years to become the world's lowest cost multi million ounce producer. Its fabulous Red Lake Gold mine is the richest gold mine on earth. Gold Corp is now the third largest gold producer in North America. This stock has been a huge moneymaker for me, just a few years ago this stock was available for four dollars and change.

Kirkland Lake Gold- This small producer hasn't been able to reach its potential. It is a consolidation of five ex-producers that produced a total of 22 million ounces in the past and has an on site 1,500-ton-per-day mill. Its proven and probable reserves are estimated at 927,000 ounces.

Klondex Mines was established in 1974 to invest in Nevada gold plays. Its portfolio currently consists of five property groups along Nevada's famous gold trends. Its prime property is the Fire Creek property, which is 15 square miles in size and is strategically located on Nevada's gold rich Battle Mountain Trend. Its outstanding share float is a modest 20,601,000 shares.

Klondike Gold- This outfit was created in 1981 to specialize in Yukon gold prospects. It has spread out since then and currently has mining claims in five different mining Camps. There are several ex-producers in these claims. At its current price you can buy the whole thing lock, stock, and barrel for about $12,800,000. I think that is way too cheap. This stock is right up my alley; it is a roll of the dice.

Moneta Gold Mines- This stock has already been commented on.

Northgate Minerals- This stock is my second favorite gold producer. Correct that, my second favorite gold and copper producer. This stock is emerging as a real powerhouse. Last year it produced 280,000 ounces of gold at a cash cost of $205 an ounce and 84.6 million pounds of copper. In addition, it acquired the Young-Davidson properties with an estimated resource of 1.5 million ounces of gold.

Pioneer Metals- I have already commented on this stock

Queenston Mining- This virtually unknown cheap blue-chip stock was incorporated in 1990 and has silently emerged as one of the giants, if not the giant, of the Kirkland Lake and Cadillac gold camps. It has wisely chosen to joint venture with other companies. It is debt free and the gold giant Newmont Mining remains an important shareholder. Its mining properties are too extensive to mention here and include several ex-producers. In the Kirkland Lake camp its land holdings extend 27 kilometers along the gold bearing Larder Lake Break. Its float is a modest 36,285,000 shares. I have been accumulating this stock since 1995. This is a stock for patient people, but it will reach the finish line.

Rubicon Minerals- This land-rich ex-producer has interests in 17 different properties, six of which are either joint ventured or optioned out. It controls 260 square kilometers of mining claims in the gold rich Red Lake Mining camp. Or as they put it: "exploring for high grade gold in the shadow of head frames in one of the world's premier gold mining camps". By the way, you are probably wondering what a head frame is? A head frame is that tower like structure that rises above the mineshaft.

St. Andrew Gold Fields- This operator is an ex-producer and a major landholder in Ontario's Timmins mining camp as well as owning properties in British Columbia and Alaska. Its Timmins property is now in preliminary production and it is struggling to find enough ore to profitably feed its mill, which is a fully operational 1,500-ton-per-day mill that was built in 1989.

Tyhee Development- This is another ex-producer that was incorporated in 1993 and is located in Canada's historic Yellowknife mining camp located in the Northwest Territories, and which produced 14 million ounces of gold. It is focusing its energies on the old Discovery Mine, which has past production of over a million ounces of gold. I fondly remember the old Discovery mine; I used to be an owner.

X Cal Resources- This is another interesting penny play in Nevada's Battle Mountain Trend it has one major property the 30-square-mile Sleeper project. Which has a very interesting location in Nevada's big game country. It has had its teeth in the Sleeper property since 1992. I like to see this type of persistence. This is my type of riverboat gamble.

There you have it, fellow riverboat gamblers, these asset rich plays are the crown jewels of gold stocks in my opinion. I think you will admit that there is an amazing amount of assets packed into these jewels. I think I have selected nothing but the best.

THE SILVER STOCKS

ABCOURT MINING .55
AVINO SILVER & GOLD 1.65
CANADIAN ZINC .57
CREAM MINERALS .45
KLONDIKE SILVER .34
MINES MANAGEMENT 5.46
NEW JERSEY MINING .68
PAN AMERICAN SILVER 16.44
SHOSHONE SILVER .18
SILVER STANDARD RES. 18.20
STERLING MINING 3.95
STILLWATER MINING 10.18

As you will recall, pure silver mines are almost nonexistent. Silver is usually found coexisting with other metals, most commonly with the base metals lead and zinc. Most of the above stocks are examples of this fact and the value of their ore bodies is primarily silver with lead and zinc being of secondary importance.

Abourt Mining- This Quebec miner was incorporated in 1971 and has five properties, two of which are ex-producers. Its prime property is the 8,526-acre Abcourt silver-zinc mine, which was a producer from 1952 to 1957 and has a mill on site. It also has the Elder mine gold project, this 1,450-acre was a producer from 1947 to 1966 and also has a mill on site.

Avino Silver & Gold- This ex-producer was incorporated in 1969 and has four properties located in Canada and Mexico. It has a very small float of only 10,697,000 shares. Its prime property is the Avino mine in Mexico, which was in production from 1974 to 2001.

Canadian Zinc- I have already commented on this stock.

Cream Minerals- I have already commented on this stock

Klondike Silver- This 27,218,000-share outfit has a current total market value of only $11,370,000 and is a spin-off I received of Klondike Gold's silver assets in the Slocan Silver Camp area in British Columbia. Klondike silver has consolidated no less than six ex-producing mines in this once vibrant silver camp. Go figure! It is obvious from the 34 cents a share price that the market neither knows nor cares about these ex silver producers. By now you know how my devious little mind works. This is a classic riverboat gambler's delight, low risk and high reward. What is the maximum downside, let's say it could fall to 10 to 20 cents a share and if silver approaches its old highs it could be a ten bagger.

Mines Management- Owns the 360-acre Montanore silver-copper mine located in northwest Montana. While the reserves aren't yet proven; the measured, indicated, and inferred tonnage is huge, an estimated ore body of about 116,586,000 tons.

New Jersey Mining- This 32,745,000 share ex silver and gold producer is located in the fabulous Couer d'Alene district in Idaho, which is the richest silver mining area ever discovered in North America. The Couer d'Alene mining region has produced over a billion ounces of silver since its discovery in the 19th century, and it is still producing.

New Jersey Mining has three ex-producers the New Jersey, the Golden Chest, and the Silver Strand. Minor production is currently underway and there is a mill on site. They need to prove up more ore. At its current rich price, it is a speculation that they will discover more ore, which is always a real possibility because they are in big game country.

Pan American Silver- This emerging south of the border silver giant has eight silver properties, six of which are in production and the last two are gearing up for production in the next two years. Production will then increase dramatically. Of course, they are currently losing money. Like I told you, the most bullish thing about silver is that at the current price almost no one can make money mining silver.

Shoshone Silver- This is another Idaho ex silver producer with 20,000,000 shares, but the public float is currently only about 5,000,000 shares. Strangely enough this prospect also has six ex-producers in its portfolio and a mill on site.

Silver Standard Resources has been a classic "asset accumulator" since 1993 when it developed its current strategy, it has been beavering away accumulating silver resources in the ground at the lowest possible cost. The annual report states that: "Silver Standard's objective is to provide shareholders with the best leverage to silver of any primary silver resource company. As such, Silver Standard's shares represent an open-ended call option on the price of silver". Silver Standard claims to have the largest "in the ground" silver reserves of any publicly traded company. It has 16 silver properties and claims more than a billion ounces in the ground, but only about 107 million ounces are in the proven and probable reserves category. As a matter of policy it refuses to consider going into production until it is convinced that the price of silver is high enough to assure profitable production. I like their strategy.

Sterling Mining- This Coeur d'Alene veteran was founded in 1903 and has recently acquired the fabulous Sunshine Mine, the greatest silver mine producer in the history of North America. The Sunshine was discovered in 1884 and has 100 miles of underground workings and a 1,000-ton-per-day mill on site. The company's mining claims cover 29,000 acres in Idaho, Montana, and Mexico. The company claims 231 million ounces of silver reserves.

Stillwater Mines- This isn't a silver mine, but it is my only palladium-platinum holding and this is as good a place as any to put it. Even though it is a producing mine, it is a continuation of my "wealth in the ground" theme. Platinum group metals, or PGMs as they are called, are incredibly rare. They are so rare that there are only two producing platinum group mines in the whole western hemisphere and Stillwater has the biggest reserves. In fact, this Montana producer has the richest known deposit of PGMs in the world. Its proven reserves in its J-M reef deposit is 42 million tons. This is absolutely huge for a platinum group deposit. Unfortunately there are about three ounces of the cheaper less desirable palladium metal for each ounce of the more desirable platinum metal in the deposit. The three biggest uses for both metals are in auto catalysts, jewelry, and as catalysts in various industrial processes.

There have been considerable problems getting their two PGM mines working smoothly. In fact, this brings up the sore point as to just who the genius was who decided to build two mines to access the same deposit. Of course they do have the excuse that the J-M reef is a 28-mile-long ore body. Incredibly, they are still losing money. This is a gamble that in the long run the ore body will overwhelm the current operational problems.

THE BASE METAL STOCKS

ADANAC MOLYBDENUM .85
BREAKWATER RESOURCES 1.00
CONSTELLATION RES. 1.37
FORMATION CAPITAL .24
GETTY COPPER .08
NORTH AMERICAN TUNGSTEN .55
PACIFICA RESOURCES .68
PALLADON VENTURES .30
POLYMET MINING 2.69
TASEKO MINING 2.49
YUKON ZINC .19

Andanac Moly- Molybdenum is an almost unknown metal. About 75% of moly world production is used as an alloy in the production of high quality steel. Among the most important of these uses is in the construction of oil and gas pipelines where it prevents corrosion and rust. The other 25% is used as a catalyst in oil refining where it removes the sulfur from sour crude oil. As with so many metals today, it is in short supply. In the last three years the price of moly has risen from $5.00 a pound to about $26.00 a pound. Adanac has four moly properties three of which are located in Nevada and have estimated total reserves of 477 million pounds. The most advanced deposit, the Ruby Creek mine, has reserves of 220 million pounds of moly and is located in British Columbia and will come on stream in 2008. You will recall that I stated that new mineral discoveries are much more rare than is popularly believed. Miners just keep going back to the same old discoveries again and again, decade after decade until they can "make it work"; the Ruby Creek deposit was first identified in 1905.

Breakwater Resources- This recovering base metal producer is now profitable and is my favorite multi-metal producer, and it has tremendous potential. It has seven mining properties and produces increasing amounts of zinc, which is its primary metal by a considerable margin, and lesser amounts of lead, copper, silver, and gold from three producing mines in British Columbia, Honduras, and Chile. A fourth mine is under development in Quebec.

Constellation Copper- This copper producer's new Lisbon mine located in Utah just started production, and believe it or not, it is the first new copper mine to go into production in the United States in the last 10 years. It has two additional mining properties in Mexico that it is trying to prove up. The price of copper has of course been skyrocketing. I am a big fan of copper, which is the prince of base metals and is indispensable in electrical wiring and plumbing. It is hard to believe, but the average home in America has 400 pounds of copper, but new homes in America because of their greater size and increased number of bathrooms have 500 pounds of copper. I know you are wondering how much copper is in a new car the answer is 50 pounds.

I don't know where the world is going to find the copper it needs if China and India reach our level of development.

Formation Capital- This Company's flagship property is the Idaho Cobalt project, which it is trying to bring into production.

This property's 2,500 acres of mining claims is the only known cobalt property in the U.S. In addition it has somehow managed to acquire, or should I say steal, the huge existing 36,000-square-foot Sunshine Precious Metal Refinery for $1,275,000. This is like Jonah swallowing the whale. The Sunshine is easily capable of producing the planned 1,500 tons of cobalt per year along with additional custom refining from local silver producers. This production would be equivalent to about 15% of current North American cobalt demand. If it succeeds, it will become America's sole integrated miner and refiner. At present it has no proven reserves, but it has measured, indicated, and inferred resources of 43.5 million pounds of cobalt and 50 million pounds of copper. Cobalt is used as a hardening alloy where high temperature performance is a must, such as in jet turbines and drill bits. Another major use is in rechargeable batteries. Formation has a portfolio of six other properties in North America and, last but not least, it has about $13,000,000 in cash. A huge amount for a company that is selling for 24 cents a share.

Getty Copper- I have already commented on this stock.

North American Tungsten- Would you believe me if I told you that this penny mining stock owns about 15% of the world's proven tungsten reserves? Hard to believe, isn't it? But it gets better; when I discovered this gem, it was selling for 18 cents a share. The story goes like this; China has for many years been the world's leading producer of tungsten. Historically it has produced about 80% of the world's tungsten. When China got its act together, it decided to eliminate some of its competition and our gem is one of the producers it drove into bankruptcy, but the sun also rises and so did tungsten prices. North American Tungsten is now back in production with an estimated 30 years of proven reserves and is the Western world's only tungsten producer. It owns two tungsten mines in the Yukon.

Pacifica Resources- I got this stock for free. It was a spin-off from Yukon Zinc. Its flagship property is the Howard's Pass 261-square-kilometer zinc property in the Yukon. According to its annual report, it is believed that the Howard Pass zinc deposits may be the largest known undeveloped zinc-lead deposits on earth. How is this for a story? The property was discovered by a joint venture between U.S. Steel and Placer Dome. These two majors spent $20 million in exploration on the property in the 1970's and in the end these geniuses got fed up with the property and sold it in 2006 for $10 million to be paid over seven years. Pretty cute, huh?

Palladon Ventures- This speculation has six properties, four of which are option properties in Argentina, which don't interest me. It has a copper property in Utah, which is of some interest. The property that interests me is its Lion Iron ore property, which is also in Utah. This property is the largest and highest-grade iron ore property located in the western United States and has been in and out of production since the 1850's.

Polymet Mining- This 4,000-acre Northmet project is the largest known undeveloped non-ferrous pollymetalic resource play in the United States and is an unusually rich copper, nickel, cobalt, and platinum deposit which is located in northeastern Minnesota. In addition it owns the huge on-site Cliff's-Erie processing mill that was built by U.S. Steel. It won't surprise you to know that all this was acquired on a 20-year lease at $75,000 per year from those geniuses at U.S. Steel. Unbelievable!

Taseko Mining owns three properties; its flagship property is the Gibraltar copper-molybdenum mine located in British Columbia. This massive 109-square-kilometer property has a 36,700-ton-per-day mill on site. Current reserves are estimated at 14.5 years and there are additional indicated reserves that could result in 30 years of production. Gibraltar was first placed into production by our old buddy Placer Dome in 1972. By 1998 when copper was selling at 61 cents a pound, they closed the mine. In due course the mine was acquired by Taseko and restarted in 2005. Copper is now selling at over $3.00 a pound and the mine is now profitable. This is a case where David ate Goliath's lunch and Goliath still hasn't figured out what happened.

Yukon Zinc- For a penny stock this is an unusually cash-rich company with $14 million in working capital. Its flagship property is the Wolverine zinc deposit in the Yukon. All together its Yukon properties come to about 695 square kilometers of mining claims. It is still in the process of proving up reserves, but its measured, indicated, and inferred resources if able to be converted into proven reserves are huge for a junior. This resource inventory comes to 3.4 billion pounds of zinc, 329 million pounds of copper, 213 million pounds of lead, 84 million ounces of silver, and 352,000 ounces of gold.

EVERYTHING ELSE

CITYXPRESS .06
CONCORD CAMERA .54
FONAR CORP. .28
IMPACT MORTGAGE 8.59
LORAL SPACE & COM 27.58
NEVADA GEOTHERM. .65
OMI CORP 21.37
RAILAMERICA 9.87
REDHAT 22.68
SPUR VENTURES .43
TERABEAM 1.81

Cityxpress- Picture this, the sicko is on the couch reading the business section of the Sunday Miami Herald. I am reading an article about a new startup called Cityxpress. I am only mildly interested until I get to the part that says that the Miami Herald has taken a position in the startup. I blast off of the couch as if I have been fired out of a cannon. Is this sick or what? Who else thinks like this? As I fire up the old computer, I realize to my horror that I am not dressed up in full riverboat gambler regalia. Ever since I made the dazzling discovery that I was a riverboat gambler and didn't know it, I have insisted on dressing for the role. After all, if you are a riverboat gambler, why not look like one? In a matter of minutes the transformation is complete. I am wearing my wonderful southern plantation hat. Clenched between my teeth is one of those cute little cigarillos that Clint Eastwood smoked in his famous spaghetti westerns. I am also wearing my classy western bola tie with the polished agate stone, which is the size of my fist, that I purchased at the world famous Tucson Gem and Mineral Show. And of course, I am wearing my impossibly gaudy huge western belt buckle. For further inspiration I mosey over to my film poster of one of Clint Eastwood's most famous Dirty Harry films, *The Enforcer.* This original film poster shows Dirty Harry walking down the street with a gun in his hand that is the size of a small cannon. Now I know what you are thinking. You are thinking: "Gee, Fred, that's the wrong film poster; Clint Eastwood didn't smoke any cigarillos in his Dirty Harry films. He only smoked cigarillos in his spaghetti westerns. You need a spaghetti western film poster." You are absolutely right of course and you have put your finger on a sore point. The spaghetti western film posters are considered classics and up to now I haven't been able to talk myself into paying the considerable price that they are asking for Clint's spaghetti western posters.

After hooking my thumbs behind my impossibly gaudy belt buckle, I now swagger over to the mirror so that I can adore myself. I am dazzled by how impossibly handsome I am but as I have already stated this isn't about how impossibly handsome I am. This is about me teaching you how to be a riverboat gambler like me, if you could ever be so lucky.

After practicing my best Clint Eastwood sneers in the mirror for only 20 minutes, I finally manage to tear myself away from the mirror. Don't laugh! I am getting better. The first time I saw myself in the mirror in my full riverboat gambler regalia, I was so dazzled by how impossibly handsome I was that it took me a full hour to tear myself away from the mirror.

Now where were we? Oh yes, the Cityxpress prospect. After one final sneer at the computer we are now ready to consider the business at hand. I have got to tell you that Cityxpress doesn't look promising. First of all I can find out almost nothing about the company. It turns out that Cityxpress is the leading supplier to the newspaper industry of event auctions. It has staged over 550 of these events and has over 350 newspapers as clients. In these event auctions, local retailers agree to auction off their goods and services in the newspaper and online in return for the exposure and to drum up business. On top of that it was a service industry with no hard assets, you know what I think of that. Only one ray of light penetrates this cathedral of gloom and darkness, the price! It was selling right in my price range 2½ cents a share. With nerves of steel the riverboat gambler makes his decision. Based on the facts I can't justify my standard ¼ of 1% to ½ of 1% of my investment capital that I allocate to my typical penny stock investments. As the ice water flows through my veins I pounce. The riverboat gambler invested 1/10th of 1% of his investment capital in Cityxpress.

This is a good opportunity to discuss some of the finer points of advanced speculation. Since I purchased the stock, it has fluctuated between 2 cents and 13 cents a share. Just contemplate the leverage of a modest purchase say in the 20,000-share to 50,000-share range and contrast that against the risk taken. Your risk capital would range between $500 and $1,250. With a 20,000-share $500-investment every ten-cent move equals $2,000. With a 50,000-share $1,250-investment every ten-cent move is equal to $5000. And yet this world, my world, is almost unknown to investors and indeed is held in total contempt.

Now I know what you are thinking. You are thinking: "Gee, Fred, what will it take to induce you to sell this investment?" Here is the way I will play it. Nothing will induce me to sell unless the stock reaches 25 cents a share, a 10 bagger. At that point I will sell 10% of my investment. Having sold 10% of my investment I will analyze the prospects for the stock and based upon my analysis, I will select price points at which I will unload varying amounts of the stock, but if I really like the stock, if I think it is a champion, an estate builder, I will do no such thing. I will do a Warren Buffet and hold it forever. If you want Warren Buffet returns, you must act like Warren Buffet. If it comes to that I will cheerfully let the stock go to zero and write it off as a tax loss. Under no circumstances will I allow myself to get blown out of my position.

Properly understood there can only be one correct strategy in the wondrous world of the riverboat gambler. A world of limited and low-cost risks and unlimited explosive profits. The sheer profit potential that exists in this scorned, ignored, and unknown world is staggering. To triumph in this world, you must be willing to do what others won't do, can't do, and indeed will regard as insane. The secret key to all this is how you deal with the downside. That is what will make or break you in my world. Let's make this concrete. I own a stock that is bouncing around like a ping-pong ball between two cents a share and 13 cents a share. Now today's Wall Street geniuses will tell you that the next time the stock tanks, I must hysterically sell the stock before it goes to zero. After all, we all know that all falling stocks are going to zero now, don't we? Brilliant! Just brilliant! This type of crazed thinking will put you in the poor house. I know; it nearly put me in the poor house.

Contemplate this! What determines my ability to make 10 or 20 times my investment in a stock like Cityxpress is my willingness to hold the stock even if it does go to zero. The next time Cityxpress tanks, it might be a launching point for a blast off to 25 or 50 cents a share. I repeat, it is my willingness to hold a stock when it is falling that will determine my ability to make super profits tomorrow. I always listen in disbelief when some so-called Wall Street authority speaks in apocalyptic terms about holding stocks that have declined by 10% to 20% as if it is the end of the world. If that is true then the world comes to an end every day on Wall Street. What fantasy land are these people living in? These types of declines are as common as dirt. Somebody needs to tell these "geniuses" that owning stocks that go down is an integral part of "adult investing". If you buy bargains, they may go down, but they won't stay down.

I knew I had arrived as an investor the first time I lost $200,000 in two months and didn't bat an eye. After all, I knew I was going to make it all back and more.

For instance as these words are being written I face the very real prospect, as I have for some time, that the price of oil could undergo a violent, short-term decline of as much as 30%. If it occurs, it is my intention to ride out this decline and perhaps add to my position. To believe in your stock picks in an age in which almost no one believes in a stock after it has fallen more than 10%, no mater how carefully they researched it, is what will determine your long-term success as an investor. After all, I did research these investments, didn't I? The alternative is to be blown out of your positions repeatedly and to wallow forever in the miserable world of chump change profits. Nobody said it was easy!

Nothing makes people happier than to take profits, and it is usually the wrong thing to do. It has truthfully been said that once a person becomes aware that he has a profit in something whether it be stock, bonds, real estate, or any other investment; it is halfway to being sold. The condo complex I live in is a perfect example of this. In the years I have lived in it, I have watched armies of people come and go at the attractive lake front condo complex I call home. As the great Florida real-estate boom rolled on, people could make substantial profits in a period as small as six months to a year in the superheated south Florida market. As soon as they realized they could cash in at a profit, these people were gone. I swear to you that some of them didn't stay around long enough to unpack. The turnover approaches insanity.

Returning to our class in advanced speculation; what is critical to understand is that when you win, you must win big. Remember this, if you throw darts, you are going to win at least 50% of the time. Let's assume you are destined to win on only 50% of your investments. What will determine how successful you are as an investor? It will be your insistence on not selling out for a chump change return in the 50% of the time that you are right and your tenacity to hold out for multiples of 100% in a world in which most people are delirious to earn a 15% return. Think about it. All stocks fluctuate. Even your most successful stock picks will have repeated price drops during your holding period. If you panic and sell them when they drop and they will drop, then you will have ended up taking huge risks for a small reward and the market will nickel and dime you forever. Any experienced investor can easily prove this fact. You only need to contemplate all the times you were blown out of your position and took a loss on a stock that you believed in. The stock didn't go to zero after you sold it, did it? With unerring instinct you sold it at or near the bottom. How do I know this, because it has happened to me so many times. The way it usually works is that within six months of your sale, the stock is selling above your purchase price. The bottom line is that this strategy which is supposed to save you from taking brutal losses will only ruin you.

Concord Camera- This is a china play, Concord has moved all its manufacturing to China. Its primary brands are Polaroid, Concord, and Keystone. It is losing money, but it is dirt-cheap. Its book value is $2.27 and its P/S ratio is way under one. In other words its annual revenues exceeds its market value.

Fonar Corp.- I own this jewel at a considerable loss, but it has great potential. It is the world leader in MRI stand up medical scanning technology, which allows patients to be scanned while they are standing or sitting up by the use of room-size scanners, and this leading technology is patent protected. The company has promise, but is currently losing money.

Impact Mortgage Holding- This position is totally out of character for me, it has no hard assets and is a service company. I think that the reason I own it is that this Mortgage REIT is one of the best managed in the business and it pays a 10% dividend.

Loral Space And Communications- This is one of my notorious "emerging from bankruptcy" plays. I purchased the junk bonds in this company after they went into default for $27 or $270 a bond. Remember that par on a bond is $100 or $1,000. The stockholders in this company were wiped out and the bondholders acquired all the stock and took over the whole company. Pretty cute, huh? I love these plays and would love to do a lot more of them, but finding the data that you need on these deals is a nightmare. Finding data on penny mining stocks is a walk in the park when compared to these deals. The company is still losing money, but business is strong and it is one of the leading satellite designers and manufacturers in the world. Both its P/S and P/B are below one.

Nevada Geothermal Power- This intriguing geothermal power play is located for good reason in Nevada, the heartland of American geothermal power. In Nevada's Great Basin region, the earth's crust is only four miles thick in comparison with a typical crust of 20 to 30 miles elsewhere. And as a result it has the highest crustal heat flow in North America. The state of Nevada currently has 14 geothermal plants operational. Nevada Geothermal currently has interests in four Great Basin properties and development drilling is underway. This is a long-term play with huge profit potential for the patient investor.

OMI Corp- This position has already been commented on.

Railamerica- Regrettably this is my only short-line railroad. I would like to own more, in particular the Genesee & Wyoming, but I can't stomach the price. What has happened is that some dark and devious investors have finally figured out what these short-line railroads are actually worth. I swear to you I can't figure out how this happened before I could establish my positions. These clowns are usually as dumb as a fence post when it comes to the obscure small caps and micro caps that are my bread and butter. In any case, this once dying 19th century industry is on the comeback trail. In a world of energy shortages, the railroads will be king. The railroads are the most energy efficient method of land transportation that exists. They are going to eat the truckers for lunch. Railamerica owns 42 short-line roads and has 8,000 miles of track. Its PE is 9.7 and its P/S and P/B is under one.

Redhat- This is the country's largest and fastest growing Linux software company. This is a rarity for me, owning a genuine growth company. I can't see anything on the horizon that will induce me to sell it. I have believed since I bought it that it was an estate builder. Of course it is outrageously overpriced, but for this baby I throw caution to the winds.

Spur Ventures- This China based phosphate producer is a play on both China and the phosphate industry, which is a critical component in chemical fertilizers.

Terabeam is a supplier to wireless networks such as Broadband and Wi Fi. It is currently losing money, but its P/S and P/B is under one.

Fred Carach

GEE, FRED, WHY DON'T YOU OWN GROWTH STOCKS?

What do you mean, "why don't I own growth stocks?" Of course I own growth stocks! Can't you count? I own four high-tech growth type stocks out of 106 positions. What is wrong with that? All right, all right, calm down. The reason that I don't own growth stocks is that I have discovered that growth stock investing doesn't work. I just got tired of having my head handed to me on a silver platter.

Over the years I have found growth stocks to be over hyped, over promoted, and worst of all, overpriced. Indeed they are priced for perfection. Unfortunately, they rarely obtain the perfection that they are priced for, and I am not the only person who has discovered this. Jeremy Siegel has written an absolutely brilliant book on this subject called *The Future For Investors* in which he gives compelling proof that against all expectations non-growth stocks in the aggregate outperform growth stocks. Another point that Jeremy hammers home in this splendid book is the critical importance of dividends for long-term investment success. As you will recall in my investing, I insist that two thirds of my investment capital be in stocks that pay a dividend of at least 6%. Thank you, Jeremy, for confirming what I had suspected. This book is must reading for its insights.

Warren Buffet is famous for never having owned a growth stock. His stock answer when asked about this is that he doesn't invest in growth stocks because he doesn't understand them. I think he is being way too modest. I think he realizes what profit destroyers these stocks are and the reason for his success is that he will have nothing to do with these toxic profit destroyers.

SOURCES AND METHODS

I get most of my ideas and information from subscribing to Barron's Financial Magazine, Forbes Magazine, and of course The Northern Miner. Yahoo's financial section is also very good and my broker, Charles Schwab, is a decent source of data. The best part of Forbes is the superb columnists section in the rear. When I receive Forbes, I start reading the columnists first and then I read the magazine from the front cover to the rear. I then read the columnists a second time to make sure I didn't miss anything. David Dreman and Jim Grant are the most outstanding. Grant's contrarian ideas are always thought provoking, even when they are wrong or just premature. I place enormous importance on independent, original, and unorthodox thinking because that is what is going to make you serious money. Thinking like every Tom, Dick, and Harry and stampeding with the herd isn't the answer. Unless the answer being sought is the road to the poor house.

I spend a lot of time in the financial section of the library. My favorite reading is the Standard & Poor reports and the superb Value Line Survey, which is a gold mine of investment data and has superb write ups. My two favorite financial letter writers are Richard Russell's *Dow Theory Letters* and Jim Dines of *The Dines Letter*. As you will discover, they are both in the hard money camp. Russell is a World War Two bombardier who served in the European theater and he has been writing his letter longer than any financial writer in existence. His letters have the well-deserved reputation of being the most interesting to read. On the international front, Jimmie Rodgers and Marc Faber are superb. I make it a point to read everything that they write.

I have been asked by one of the reviewers of this work to comment on how much my experiences as a commercial real estate appraiser have shaped my attitude as a stock market investor. I want to thank Carlos for making me consider this fact. My initial reaction was none at all, but as I thought the matter through, I realized that it had a considerable impact that I have only just become aware of. I guess the best place to start is one day early in my career when I was driving home in my car. I was very discouraged and considering a career change. As I thought through the possibilities, the answer I came up with was to become a Gemologist. As soon as the answer occurred to me, I started laughing. I remember thinking: "Boy what a sicko you are!" For those of you who don't know, a Gemologist is an appraiser who is licensed to appraise gems. As I thought the matter through I realized for the very first time that I was obsessed with knowing what the market value of things were, whether it was real estate, stocks, or gem stones.

Here is what commercial real estate appraising taught me about appraising stocks. If you stop to think about it, appraising commercial real estate is a lot like appraising corporations. In appraising we are taught that there are three approaches to estimating market value. They are called the income approach to value, the comparable sales approach to value (also known as the market approach), and the cost approach to value. We are all taught that when appraising commercial real estate, the income approach to value is usually the most valid approach because commercial real estate is purchased because of the income stream that it generates. The comparable sales approach and the cost approach to value are regarded as supporting indicators of value and should reinforce the conclusion of the income approach to value. This certainly made sense to me, at least at first.

Let's start with the core of the income approach, the stabilized operating statement. The statement begins at the top of the page with the estimate of the potential gross income that the property could generate if all rentals received were at current market rents and the occupancy rate was 100%. From this figure you subtract the all-important vacancy and collection loss and you proceed from there to subtract all expenses until you get to the key figure, the net operating income that the subject property can generate. This is the figure that will enable you to estimate what the property is worth.

The problem begins when you receive the alleged income and expense statements from the owner. I almost never received a totally accurate statement. Most of them were jokes. The problem begins on the second line, the vacancy and collection loss line. You would think that this would be pretty straightforward? Guess again! The problem isn't with the vacancy rate, but whether or not the tenants are paying the rent that is indicated on the lease. You would be amazed at how often this isn't the case. Rest assured the owner won't enlighten you about all this. The base rent is usually paid. The problem comes with the rent escalators, the CPI index clause increases and the real-estate taxes pass throughs that the tenant is supposed to pay.

It is amazing how often they aren't paid. In fact you could almost call them wish clauses. Everything of course depends on how strong the owner thinks the rental market is. If the market is strong, the owner will demand that the tenant pay the full lease rent.

I am reminded of one commercial owner in the Little Havana area of Miami who I represented for years as a property tax appeal agent. Each year I would challenge the tax assessments on his commercial properties before the special master and endeavored, with a considerable amount of success, to get his real estate taxes reduced. In one case the Peruvian, as I referred to him since that is where he came from, was moaning to me about how he had been cheated on a 16-unit commercial plaza that he had just purchased. A flourishing restaurant occupied four of these units. When he received his first rental check from the restaurant he was shocked to discover that the check was considerably less than what the lease stated. When he confronted the restaurant owner, he was informed that the restaurant owner had never paid what the lease indicated and had no intention of starting now. The previous owner had been informed that the restaurant owner couldn't or wouldn't pay the indicated rental increases and the prior owner had acquiesced. You would be amazed at how common this is unless you are dealing with national tenants. The Peruvian asked me if I thought he was doing the right thing by letting the restaurant owner get away with this. I told him that he was doing the right thing. He simply couldn't afford to lose his star tenant. The four units could easily have stood vacant for months and the replacement tenants would probably demand considerable repairs and improvements to the units and might not have the staying power of the restaurant.

Then there is the whole business of repairs and other necessary expenses that somehow never manage to appear on the expense statement. My favorite category is the category called "reserves for replacements" that appears on the income statement after the fixed operating expenses and variable operating expenses have been subtracted. This category is for the required annual set aside to replace long life items like the roof and central air-conditioning which will need to be replaced in the future. You would be amazed at how many real-estate investors aren't even aware that they need to deduct these charges before they can get a true indication of how much their property is really earning. Things get really ugly when the appraiser has to explain to these alleged professionals that their property isn't worth what they say it is.

I think it is safe to say that the buyer of any investment property who receives in his first year of ownership what he has been led to believe he was going to receive should drop to his knees and thank God for a miracle.

The bottom line is that I learned that I couldn't rely on the income statement to establish the value of the subject property unless it was supported by the other two approaches to value. As time progressed I realized that the comparable sales of similar commercial properties were a far more accurate indicator of market value than the flawed income approach as long as comparable sales were available.

Notice the similarities to analyzing corporations. The income or reported earnings is suspect, but not the price per square foot of comparable real-estate sales, which is of course comparable to the assets of a corporation. In other words, appraise assets and not deceitful income.

THE TRIUMPH OF THE STUPIDS

Now I know what you are thinking. You are thinking: "Gee, Fred, when are you going to tell us about your real-estate speculations? The sad truth of the matter is that they are almost nonexistent. Except for the roof over my head and four interesting timeshare weeks that I now own on beach front property in the Ft. Lauderdale area, there are none. It was my great misfortune to live through what was probably the greatest sustained real-estate bull market in history. The great south Florida real-estate boom that was born in 1991 and finally died in 2006. This market was relentless. It wouldn't go down. Except for a profitable rental condo that I owned for 17 years and one foreclosure deal and two property flips, there was nothing.

I was left at the starting gate. I don't do the greater fool theory. I either buy bargains or I don't buy at all. And during the

Florida real-estate boom bargains didn't exist. I know, I couldn't find any. This is seldom understood, but the professional investor is always at a great disadvantage in any sustained boom. He knows what stocks or real estate is worth or at least he did know until the crazies showed up and commenced their insane bidding wars. The tendency of the professional when he sees stocks or real estate skyrocket beyond reason is to step aside and let the amateurs play their stupid little games. In due course they will have their heads handed to them on a silver platter and the professionals will then be able to cash in.

What I didn't realize was that I was witnessing the triumph of the stupids. The triumph of the greater fool theory. They were riding one of the greatest bull markets in history. A bull market that seemed like it would never end. They were riding a wave that they couldn't lose on.

I remember the day when I finally realized that it was hopeless. I had long since given up on foreclosure auctions. The stupids were relentless in engaging in their bidding wars. They drove everything, and I do mean everything, far above market value. Their attitude was that if it was selling at foreclosure, it had to be a bargain. No matter what it ended up selling for.

I had carefully researched three vacant lots that were being auctioned off at a tax deed sale. These sales are almost unknown by the general public and I thought there might be an opportunity there. I was wrong. Two of the lots sold for twice my estimate of market value, and the third lot sold for three times my estimate of market value. The triumph of the stupids was now complete, but the sun also rises. The time of the stupids has now ended. And the time of the professionals has begun.

I now realize that what I should have done was to move to some decaying rust belt city with a population that was either stagnant or declining. In such an environment the greater fool practitioner isn't rewarded. He is wiped out. The professional can wheel and deal in such a city without engaging in bidding wars with amateurs.

MY FIFTEEN MINUTES OF FAME

It all started very innocently. I just wanted to know if it made tax sense to convert my IRA account into a Roth IRA at my age. So I contacted the Miami Herald's financial consultant by email and asked for advice. The lady told me that this was more complicated than I imagined. I was informed that I would need to do a "money makeover". I agreed to do the "money makeover".

After the form arrived, I realized that there were going to be more problems than I anticipated. After I got over the amazing number of questions that they were asking me, there was an additional problem. They had thoughtfully provided me with 12 spaces on the form to list my stock holdings. This was going to be a major problem. It wasn't fair of me to expect the financial planner to try to analyze my 100 plus portfolio of stocks that I was sure she had never heard of, and I knew she would never be able to handle my penny mining stocks. I had a mental vision of her doing a triple somersault and bouncing on her head three times if she saw these little gems. For various reasons, I have four accounts at Charles Schwab. The solution was to only list my holdings in my two IRA accounts. The only stocks in my IRA accounts were my income plays.

In due course I was invited to the certified financial planner's Coral Gables office for the interview. Seated at the conference table were the Miami Herald's financial consultant and the certified financial planner who had done my "money makeover". As the interview proceeded, I realized that they were dazzled by me. They were having a hard time figuring out how somebody who had never earned serious money in his life had managed to accumulate what I had. They were curious about how I had discovered things like oil & gas royalties and Canadian Income Trusts. I was being stared at as if I had just arrived by spaceship from Mars. The interview was professional and pleasant enough. I was told what I had expected to hear. That I had been lucky up to now and that I was dangerously concentrated in REITs and the oil & gas industry, and that I needed to diversify much more across sectors.

After the interview was over, I was presented with a very impressive comprehensive financial plan book of more than 100 pages and I finally received the only information that I was interested in hearing. It turns out that at my age it didn't make sense to convert my IRA into a Roth IRA. Now I know what you are thinking. You are thinking: "Gee, Fred, where are you going with all this?" Relax! I am getting there. The next day, out of the blue, I received a phone call from the Miami Herald, they informed me that they wanted to send a photographer over to take pictures. Isn't that unusual? I asked. I never remembered seeing the photo of someone asking for financial advise in the newspaper. They responded that because my case was so interesting, they wanted to take some photos in case they wanted to do more than usual. This was the first time that I knew that there was anything interesting about my case. I had a hard time figuring out what was interesting or special about the simple question that I wanted answered. In for a penny, in for a dollar.

The photographer came over and took about a million pictures of me. I asked him if he wasn't going a little overboard with the photos. He told me that this was standard procedure. I didn't hear anything more from them for a couple weeks and I thought that the whole matter was over. Then on Sunday morning October 16, 2005 I was on my couch reading the Miami Herald when I turned to the front page of the Miami Herald's financial section I was blown away to discover staring back at me a large color photo of myself. A two-page article with a total of eight columns accompanied my photo. I was thunderstruck. I couldn't believe it. Boy, I really am handsome.

The article concentrated on how frugal I was and suggested that I was way too concentrated in REITSs and the oil & gas industry; and that I needed to do some serious sector diversifying. They were impressed with how much I had accumulated on my modest income and presented me as an example of what could be achieved by a combination of tenacity and frugality. I couldn't help thinking that if they had seen my whole portfolio with its penny mining stocks, that they would have really freaked out. The article left the clear impression that I needed to lighten up and spend some money.

Now we are finally getting to the point of all this. There was absolutely nothing wrong with their advice. It is the standard, plain vanilla financial advice that any financial consultant is going to recommend. And for the typical investor who spends his life being jerked around by the touts, useful advice. My problem was that it was way too basic for me. To put it bluntly, I don't conform to conventional investment doctrine. In a 10,000 stock universe, I think that the blind adoration devoted to the "Nifty Fifty" and the S&P 500 is just plain nuts. And it is more than that; it is a contemptible cop out. I have already commented on the "Nifty Fifty," the S&P 500 and the notorious Random Walk Theory. Taken together this unholy trinity has a strangle hold on conventional, accepted investment wisdom that is nearly absolute and extends from the college campus to Wall Street. I have more problems with this theory than you can shake a stick at.

What you have got to understand is that there is a reason for all this. Let's give it a name. Let's call it the "Career Protection Act" for Wall Street professionals. As we already know, the street's entire investment complex is geared to beating the S&P 500 on a quarterly basis. The fact that there is a 10,000 stock universe out there is resolutely ignored by the Street; and there is a very good reason for this. Under this carefully contrived "career protection" racket it is possible for almost everyone to look good. If you look at the performance of the pros, you can't help but notice that everyone is clustered in a tight grouping right around the performance of the S&P 500. Surprise! Surprise! By basing everyone's performance on a small 500 stock universe and by compressing the reporting period to a ludicrous series of short, repeating 90-day time periods, it takes real talent to look bad.

This scheme, as stupid as it is, does a wonderful job of doing what it was designed to do. It protects the Wall Street professional. Think about it. How far wrong can you go in 90 days using this system? As I have already pointed out because the S&P 500 is capitalization-weighted index, it is possible to mimic the S&P 500 with as little as about 12 of the largest capitalization stocks. The consequences of capitalization weighting in an index are enormous. In a recent article the highly regarded Forbes columnist, Laszlo Birinyi, stated that the current weighting for the largest S&P 500 stock was an amazing 177 times that of the smallest stock in the index.

Then you artfully throw in a bunch of hot momentum plays to show everyone how "clued in" you are to today's most popular plays and you have it made.

Under this carefully contrived system the distance between the best and the worst is very small indeed, which is just what was intended. It is beyond dispute that this system serves the needs of the Wall Street professional. After all, using this system they can all look good. The $64,000 question is: does it serve the needs of the investor? I don't think so! If you take your eyes off of the S&P 500, which you aren't supposed to do, you will find out that there are tons of small caps out there that outperform the S&P 500 every year. Rest assured that the so-called Wall Street professionals aren't going to inform you of this. Why, you might have the nerve to ask all kinds of embarrassing questions.

There is one more issue left to consider. And that is the Street's flat refusal to commit to any kind of investment discrimination between the various sectors. They will proudly inform you that they are too stupid to know what sectors will outperform the market and therefore you should buy everything. How convenient! Guess what! This gutless failure on their part is trumpeted as a virtue. They will proudly inform you that this is proof of how shrewd they are as investors. They are far too clever to commit themselves on what sectors will outperform. Pretty cute, huh? The virtue of this strategy is that they can never be proven wrong. You have got to admit that these people are certainly aware of their "limitations". I ask you what other profession can get away with something like this? You have got to admire these people's modesty and their gall. Then again, they have much to be modest about, don't they? What other profession can constantly proclaim that they are dumber than a fence post unless the fence post is having a bad day? And then be rewarded for their proudly proclaimed ignorance with an income that the rest of us would kill for.

Why, just the other day I was watching one of these fearless professionals being interviewed on CNBC. The interviewer was starring in wide-eyed awe as the "professional" recommended the purchase of IBM, Microsoft, and Coke.

You must be a genius! You must be a genius! Why in a million years it would never have occurred to me to invest in these hitherto "unknown stocks". Let me write down these names before I forget them. I was ready to lose my cookies. This "genius" makes considerably more in a month than I make in a year.

You have got to ask yourself a serious question. Who is the real professional? Is the real professional someone who only recommends Nifty Fifty stocks about which everybody and his brother already know? Or is the real professional someone who has done his own independent research and is willing to recommend stocks that no one has ever heard of?

I am not a happy camper where the Street is concerned. I am having none of their decades-long outrageous and contemptible scams. I have a secret dream. My secret dream is to haul a .50 caliber machine gun up the stairwell of the New York Stock Exchange and send these swine to the Promised Land that they so richly deserve. I am of course thinking of hell.

Now I know what you are thinking. You are thinking: "Gee, Fred, those babies weigh a ton. It is going to be a nightmare to drag one of those monsters up the stairwell. Why not settle for a .30 caliber light machine gun? It has been around since at least the Second World War and has a well-deserved reputation for getting the job done?" You are absolutely right of course. The problem is that the .30 caliber wouldn't blow a big enough hole in the bastards. After four decades of watching them sell their snake oil and get away with it, you have no idea how personal this has become.

My digression is over with. The point that I have been trying to drive home is this. Is it really a brilliant strategy to recommend Nifty Fifty stocks and to refuse to commit to any investment sector which is the unchallenged orthodox belief? Or is it just a gutless cop out? Is it possible that humans are so stupid that it is impossible to beat the indexing craze? You decide!

For myself, this decision was made many years ago. I have carefully outlined the reasons for concentrating nearly all my firepower in a handful of carefully chosen sectors. I am a veteran of more than four decades on one of the most unforgiving battlegrounds on earth. The battleground of investment survival, and I have the battle scars to prove it. I have chosen my path and if I am right, the rewards will be huge.

SUMMING UP

Well fans there you have it. I have carefully selected 106 gems for your careful consideration. The rest of what I own are Leaps and won't be listed. I just hope that the reader has learned as much from reading this work as I have learned from writing it. This voyage of discovery has forced me to crystallize and think out beliefs and convictions to their bottom, which hitherto had probably existed mostly in my subconscious. For me the most remarkable discovery was of course that I was a riverboat gambler and didn't know it. This was a dazzling discovery to me and I am sure it will be a dazzling discovery to my friends and family when they find out about it. I just hope they don't fall down laughing. The proof, however, is in the eating of the pudding, just take a gander at the stuff I own and ask yourself who else but a riverboat gambler would own this stuff? There isn't a blue chip in the lot. Consider this, if you showed 98% of the world's investors the list of the companies I own, with the exception of perhaps two stocks, they wouldn't have heard of a single name on the list. And if they showed you a list of the companies that they own, it would look like a wasteland of "Nifty Fifty" companies. I am of course the anti-blue-chip investor and the champion of small-cap and micro-cap investing.

I want to leave you with my favorite quote from Napoleon:

There are many good generals in Europe but they see too many things. I see only the decisive thing.

Here is how I interpret Napoleon's statement. In life we are all bombarded with a never-ending blizzard of alleged facts or truths. Some of these alleged facts are of course false, but far more important are the great deceivers. Those facts that are both true and also irrelevant. And lastly there are the facts that are both true and decisive. Life is a never-ending struggle of trying to isolate from this blizzard of facts those facts that are both true and decisive. If we can do that, our victories on the battlefield of life will be assured. There is no arena of battle where being able to grasp the decisive facts is more rewarding than in the stock market. It will make you rich. This work has been an attempt to introduce to the reader the stock market facts that I believe are decisive. And just what is the decisive thing on the blood splattered battleground where I choose to hang out? It is buying assets at bargain prices and holding them. Nothing else works over the long term. And I have the battle scars to prove it. Let's do one last conversation:

"Why did you buy that stock?"

"Because it was going up."

"Why did you then sell that stock?"

"Because it was going down."

"When did it start going down?"

"Right after I bought it."

"How long did it take the stock to turn around after you sold it and sell for a price that was higher than what you bought it at?"

"About six months!"

"How long have you been committing these stupidities?"

"Since I started investing."

The loser is a chaser who is forever chasing the latest news and trends. Trends that are here today and gone tomorrow. The brilliant strategy of these losers is to take today's news and trends and then project them forever into the future. This cute and clever strategy guaranties that they will be jerked around by the market forever, like a monkey on a chain.

The winner knows that this strategy has as much substance as smoke. The winner purchases assets at bargain prices. If he does that, the trend will take care of itself.

Consider this, the loser is always one loss from being out of business entirely. Imagine that a new stock investor makes a profit of $50,000 on his first trade and loses $20,000 on his second trade. How probable is it that there will ever be a third trade? In my estimation, it is very improbable that there will ever be a third trade. People's tolerance for loss is much lower than is commonly believed. In short, what will happen, and happen repeatedly, is that people, who if they would only stick to the discipline would be successful long-term investors, are panicked out of investing because they can't tolerate a big loss, even if they are way ahead of the game.

Another point that requires summing up is how obscene and degenerate today's stock market is. I think it isn't outrageous to claim that the stock market today in its attitudes, beliefs, and structure is a threat to the long-term viability of capitalism. The stock market today is in reality a vampire that is feeding on corporate America. It makes obscene demands that no real corporation competing in the real world can meet for any sustained period. And it then exacts its brutal punishment on them when they fail, and in the end they must all fail. Its imbecilic demand that the only measuring stick of corporate performance is the next quarter's earnings number forces corporations to engage in unhealthy short-term and shortsighted practices that can only harm the long-term health and viability of both the corporation and the capitalist system itself. It has reached the point where corporations are reluctant to engage in long-term planning and to make new capital investments because they know it will hurt the next quarter's numbers.

As an investor I look back on more than four decades. The transformation of both Wall Street and the investing public during this period has been astounding, and not for the better. I fondly hearken back to a world in which investors regarded themselves as owners of a corporation and not as owners of a lottery ticket. These owners took pride in the corporations that they owned and they bought stock with the intention of holding their positions for at least five or ten years. Their attitude was that if you aren't willing to commit to a corporation for at least that long, what was the point in buying it? A healthy dividend was a core investment principle. Stock holders were far more interested in receiving a healthy dividend and seeing that dividend increased over the years than they were with the quarterly numbers, which they correctly regarded as being transitory and of little long-term consequence. Capital gains in this world were regarded as being the icing on the cake, but they weren't the cake. In such a world corporations could routinely exceed investor expectations because investors had reasonable expectations of what a corporation could deliver.

To sum up, the typical investor back then was just that, an investor with a long-term investment horizon. This sane and sound investment world is now in ruins and we are all the poorer because of it. Today's so-called investor isn't an investor at all. He is a short-term trader with a time horizon that never exceeds one unfavorable quarterly number. The prognosis for the investment success of these sunshine warriors isn't good; it is terrible.

We now live in a world of investor insanity, a world in which impossible growth demands are being made on corporate America. We have armies of idiots today who demand that big-cap corporations grow at 15% a year; an impossible demand. As I have been at pains to point out, the bigger a corporation becomes, the more its growth rate must resemble that of the nation. Trust me, we aren't growing at 15% a year; we struggle to grow at 4% a year.

Just the other day I was in my car listening to a caller whining on a financial program about the performance of General Electric. He was recounting the considerable virtues of this superbly managed company and he couldn't understand how a company with so many virtues as he put it couldn't get out of its own way. Why, he asked, was it like climbing Mount Everest for the stock to go up a dollar? The answer fool is because General Electric is the economy! In my world, all big caps are of course has-beens by definition.

Sound fundamental analysis as preached by Graham & Dodd and uber investor Warren Buffet is practiced by fewer and fewer investors, in spite of its proven success. And strangely enough this makes sense. There is no investment process that will work when your time horizon never exceeds past 90 days. Sound stock analyzing has been replaced by the mindless, infantile, knee jerk response to all the news that is reported over the news wires. It is taken for granted that all the news is both equally valid and is also of cosmic importance, and therefore requires an immediate buy or sell order.

The market, as never before in its history, has assumed the deranged character of a perpetual "overreaction machine". As ever-greater armies of so-called investors stampede in unison in response to this news, the result is ever-greater volatility in stocks as they are jerked up and down for no valid reason with ever-greater violence.

In such a world, the value player is king. It is only necessary for him to wait and the market will deliver to him the type of "in the gutter" bargains that in the old days were very rare.

That is it, fellow riverboat gamblers; the introduction to my world is over. I hope you found it strange and wondrous. I also hope you decide to enter it. The rewards can be huge. And don't forget to buy that wonderful southern plantation hat, it helps to dress for the role. And save a place for me on the Mississippi Belle. I can be reached at FCA4980633@aol.COM.

Fred Carach

Forty Years a Speculator

Fred Carach

Forty Years a Speculator

Made in the USA
Lexington, KY
16 February 2011